WEALTH
ON YOUR PAYCHECK

WEALTH
ON YOUR PAYCHECK

The guerrilla savings plan
for getting out of debt,
staying out of debt,
and getting rich!

By D. Calvin Trout

International Publishing Corporation
Chicago

Library of Congress Number: 91-71589

ISBN 0-942641-36-1

Note: In the interest of clarity, the pronoun *he* is used only in the absence of a generic singular pronoun signifying both he and she. This is in no way intended as a discriminatory practice; it simply makes for easier, less awkward writing and reading.

This publication is designed to provide accurate and authoritative information in regard to the subject matter covered. It is sold with the understanding that the author and publisher are not engaged in rendering legal, accounting or other professional service. If legal advice or other expert assistance is required, the services of a competent professional person should be sought. (From a declaration of principles jointly adopted by a committee of the American Bar Association and a committee of publishers).

Cover design: Al Trungale & Associates

To

The Ultimate Power

My Wife Puja (The Princess)

My Son Victor

And My Friend Al

Table
of Contents

Author's Note   1

Chapter 1 / Who Should Read This Book?   3

    WHY AM I WRITING THIS BOOK?   5
    SOCIAL SECURITY = FALSE SECURITY   6
    IF WE DID IT, ANYONE CAN   8
    WHAT THIS BOOK IS ABOUT   9

Chapter 2 / Confessions of an Ex-Credit Card Junkie   11

    JUST 48 EASY PAYMENTS . . .   12
    LOTS OF CHECKS, NO BALANCE   14
    A NEW TWIST ON OLD BEHAVIOR   15
    TWO DISASTERS = AN OPPORTUNITY   17
        Learning the Hard Way: The Lessons My Depression-
            Era Parents Tried in Vain To Teach Me   18
        From Big Money to Instant Poverty in
            Ten Seconds   19
        Toughing It Out   21
    A FRESH START   23
        Keeping Track of Our Progress   23
    OUT OF WORK AGAIN—BUT SMARTER   25
        Running Our Household Like a Business   25
    FROM DEBT TO SUBSTANTIAL EQUITY   26

Chapter 3 / Getting Started: Knowing Your Financial Situation   29

CHARTING YOUR COURSE   31
WHY THE RICH GET RICHER   37
THE GIFT WEDDING DRESS   41
THE RIGHT ATTITUDE   42

Chapter 4 / Washing Ziploc® Bags: A Guide to Guerilla Savings   45

CONVENIENCE IS EXPENSIVE   46
BLUE WATERS = MONEY DOWN THE DRAIN   48
   Odor Overkill   48
   Do It Yourself   49
   The Price of Fear   49
WASHING ZIPLOC® BAGS   50
USE TIME TO YOUR ADVANTAGE   53
   Deals Staring Us in the Eye   54
DEVELOPING X-RAY VISION   55
   Separating Fool's Gold from 24 Karat   57
WAREHOUSING: HOW TO AMPLIFY BARGAINS   60
   Must Be a Party   61
EVERYTHING IS NEGOTIABLE   62
   The Pen Is Mightier   65
   Hit 'Em Where They Hurt   66
BECOME A GROCER'S NIGHTMARE   68
   Rebates—Wringing Out the Last Nickel   69

Chapter 5 / From Poor Immigrant to Rich Citizen in Ten Years or Less   71

THEY LAUGHED WHEN I ASKED HOW THEY DID IT   71

Getting Maximum Value   73
It's Better if It's Free   77
Gambling—Sucker's Style? Or Winner's?   78
HOW NOT TO BE PENNY WISE AND
        POUND FOOLISH   80
TAKING THE HEAT OUT OF UTILITY BILLS   81
AUTOMATIC SPENDING   83
WASTE NOT, WANT NOT   85
HOW FRESH IS FRESH IS FRESH?   86
NO EASY WAY   87

**Chapter 6 / Your Annual Budget: Blueprint
        for Success   89**

HAVING A BUDGET DOESN'T MEAN YOU HAVE
        TO LIVE ON MACARONI AND CHEESE   89
HOW TO GET STARTED   91
TRANSLATING THE PAST INTO THE FUTURE   98
PROFITS P-L-E-A-S-E ...   105
        Beyond the Numbers   110
KEEPING TRACK TO STAY ON TRACK   110
        Learning How To Pay Your Bills   113
SOMETIMES IT'S BETTER TO BORROW   114
BUDGETING IS NO FUN ... OR IS IT?   116

**Chapter 7 / Long-Range Planning: When You Wish
        Upon a Star   119**

WHY DIDN'T I THINK OF THAT?   119
TAKING THE LONG VIEW   120
WHERE TO START?   125
CREATING MONEY CONSCIOUSNESS   129

Chapter 8 / What To Do with Your Savings: The Basics 131

A GOOD RETURN FOR A SAFE INVESTMENT 131
    The Three Little Pigs 133
CASH INSTRUMENTS 136
MORE SOPHISTICATED INVESTMENTS 137
    The Biggest Investment You'll Ever Make 138
    Rent or Buy, Which is Better? 139
    Negotiating Real Estate Deals 140
    Empty Houses = Potentially Good Deals 141
    Creativity, P-l-e-a-s-e 142
HOW AM I DOING? 143

Chapter 9 / The Reality of Taxes 145

THE MOOD OF CONGRESS 145
WHAT YOU CAN DO TO REDUCE YOUR TAXES 150
    Rental Property Deductions—Watch Out 154
    Consumer Debt Deduction . . . Going, Going,
        Gone 154
    Educational Expenses—New Slant on an Old
        Problem 155
PAY TAXES WHEN YOUR INCOME IS LOWER 156
TAX-FREE INCOME 157
MEDICAL AND MISCELLANEOUS DEDUCTIONS 159
THE EARNED INCOME CREDIT 163
HOW TO KEEP YOUR TAXES FROM GETTING
    BIGGER 163

**Chapter 10 / Survival Solutions for Credit
        Kamikazes   165**

        FIRST STEPS   166
        WHEN YOU CAN'T MAKE IT TO THE NEXT
            PAYCHECK   167
        EARNINGS ALTERNATIVES   170
        DO A DONALD TRUMP . . . SELL YOUR ASSETS   171
        WHEN HIDING YOUR CAR WON'T HELP   171
        THE DOWNSIDE OF BANKRUPTCY   174

Chapter 11 / Attitudes for Success   177

        DO YOU HAVE AN EARNING OR SPENDING
            PROBLEM?   177
        THE THIRD TIME'S A CHARM   178
        THE ATTITUDES FOR FINANCIAL SUCCESS   180
        THE SUCCESSES OF OTHERS   181
        THE LAW OF RETURNING COMPENSATION   182
        GO FOR IT!   183

Suggested Reading   185

Sources   189

Author's Note

Fifteen years ago, if anyone had told me that some day I would write a book telling others how they could become wealthy, I would have called him a lunatic. I would have said, "Me? A card-carrying member of the working poor? How could I tell anyone anything about money?" I would have explained how I had never saved a nickel and how I could barely make the payments on my modest two-bedroom house and three-year-old economy car.

Sound familiar? Well I'm here to tell you that if your story sounds anything like mine, you can escape the world of "barely making it" and have the American Dream. You *can* become wealthy on your paycheck. Many have done it before you. Many are actively doing it today . . . including me!

I've discovered a system that can propel you to a new world of financial freedom. A system that will catapult you into the world of the rich. I know it works because I've done it myself. I have gone from near bankruptcy to the threshold of millionairedom in a relatively short time using legal, honest, and low-risk strategies.

The methods and tactics I describe in *Wealth on Your Paycheck* I call guerilla savings. I use the term guerilla savings because financial success is really a war. It has winners, losers, casualties—and fatalities. To win this war, you have to fight for your share. Many determined forces will oppose you. For them your success is their failure. You must develop mental toughness

2 Wealth on Your Paycheck

to win. You must keep a code of secrecy and come blazing over the next hill like John Wayne. You must have faith and demand the success.

Most of all, you must plan, scheme, and continuously study your enemy.

At one time or another, I have used every technique in this book. I know they work, but I also know that sometimes they don't succeed on the first try. For example, some merchants may find my buying tactics objectionable. Others may refuse to cooperate and may even try to make you feel guilty for protecting your own interest. If they do, leave their stores immediately!

There are always people who'll do business with you on your terms, but you may have to seek to find them. All religions exhort their followers to "seek and find," but few followers take the advice. Those who do often become discouraged and give up when things don't go immediately their way. Only the very few who plod on against all odds win. And believe me, eventually they do win!

Remember this is warfare. Skirmishes as well as battles need to be won. For the winners the booty is wealth beyond imagination!

I dedicate this book to you. I want you to succeed! Your success is important to me and all Americans. Our dream is built upon those who have succeeded. You are building the next generation's dream. So fasten your seat belts. Let's get started on your road to riches.

CHAPTER 1

Who Should Read This Book?

Are you sick and tired of being broke? Then this book is for you. For you who no matter how much you earn never seem to make enough to get ahead. For you, the "working poor," who expend all your energies just to stand still.

This book is also written for those who have had the slightest inkling that they could make it big. And for those who have dreamed of magnificent success. And for those who would like to know how it feels to live a debt-free-life—one that lets them enjoy life's luxuries without worrying about how to pay for them.

But this book is especially written for you who looked at the book's cover or contents page and growled. "Impossible. Stupid. Absurd. . . ." You need this book more than all others, because you have turned off your mind to possibility. You've given up hope, and although you did it for what you believe are good reasons . . . YOU'RE WRONG!

Before us is a great period of opportunity: Opportunity resulting from dramatic world changes. A huge market has emerged, and for the wise and financially able this market offers the possibility of massive wealth beyond imagination!

The old saying is that it takes money to make money. It's true. And the *more* money you have the easier it is to make it. For example, you can make a million dollars without any effort at all. Here's how: In an account with an interest rate of 7.5%

one million dollars will double in value in 9 years and 3 months. Just like that you've made a million dollars.

What an enviable position to be in: Money making money for you without your working for it. But before we get too carried away with the idea we have to address the basic problem: How do we make the first million! The purpose of this book is to teach you how.

My old pessimistic friend Walter used to scowl at financial self-help books. He claimed that no one will tell you the secret of making money. He used to say, "Why would anyone who really had that kind of knowledge share it? Why wouldn't he just keep it to himself?" So why am I telling you my secrets?

I have some basic reasons for sharing my discoveries in this book. The most basic is that your future and mine are intertwined. We need each other. Our own well-being and our nation's existence as a major world power depend on our thoughts, our choices, and our actions.

It's no news that the U.S. is struggling to maintain its economic leadership in the world. In some industries we've already lost our lead. With the setbacks has come a new national disease. We've been drained of hope. It's obvious in the defensive, protectionistic news reports we hear and read daily. The "news" preys on our fears that we may lose our jobs and our property to foreign interests. We are fed a constant diet of bad business news and are hammered with reports of bankruptcies and business failures. Good news is whispered on the back pages of newspapers.

Perhaps the biggest and most important thing we've lost is our national pride and determination. We've lost our "Can Do" attitude, the attitude that pulled us out of the worst economic setback this country has ever seen—the Great Depression of the 1930s. The same energy supported us through World War II. The same spirit carried our flag to the moon and helped us recover from the tragic losses of our national heroes

Kennedy and King. America the invincible, the strong—where are you?

Our current pessimism is sapping our vitality, sucking the life force out of us, and unless we change our attitudes, the force and vigor that made this nation great will disappear. And with it will go our wonderful standard of living.

Many developing nations are standing in line just to taste the magnificent opportunities we have. I work with many international businesspeople in publishing and commercial trade shows. Over the years I've seen the enormous enthusiasm foreign businesspeople have for this country. The eyes with which they look at America see hope and promise. They expect and usually do profit greatly from their investment here in time, energy, and money.

Their countries support them with a ready pool of capital to grow their businesses. This capital comes from either government subsidies or the combined assets of thousands of individual savers. Countries like Japan have both.

Instead of ready capital for our businesses, though, we have massive debt! And not just the deficit debt we hear about in the news: We also have the cumulative weight of billions in consumer debt. Americans save less than 6% of their total earnings, compared to 16% for the average Japanese wage earner.

The low savings rate combined with the national debt strains available funds for industrial expansion. It makes loans too expensive for business borrowing, causing businesses to stop growing. The result is fewer jobs, market share lost to foreign products, and smaller raises and bonuses.

WHY AM I WRITING THIS BOOK?

I'm writing for my own selfish reasons. I cannot succeed entirely on my own. To succeed the way I envision, I need a booming country. For that to happen, capital is needed for growth! That means attitudes must change. Your money must join mine to build an economy that will blossom. With it will come not only jobs, raises, and cheaper goods but also a skyrocketing stock market, world economic dominance, and continued good times.

As proof I offer Japan, a country whose products no less than 30 years ago were regarded as JUNK! Now it has 5% to 10% national growth, an exploding stock market, and 140 jobs for every 100 applicants. It can happen again here. We just must believe it and prepare for it! "Can Do" may be corny but it works!

SOCIAL SECURITY = FALSE SECURITY

Another reason I'm writing this book is to help people realize that as some of us approach old age we are teetering on the brink of disaster. As one of the oldest members of the baby boom generation, and a student of population statistics, I am painfully aware of how inadequate our Social Security system is.

Right now a large majority of workers financially support a minority of retired Americans. Although for the first time in decades the system is solvent, it is frighteningly expensive! With worker and employer contributions at 15% of the first $53,400 in 1991 a worker earns (and rising), a huge portion of our wages is needed to keep the system afloat.

Back in the early Seventies when I started my first job, my employer laughed about Social Security when I asked what my deductions would be. After explaining the amounts that would be withheld for federal taxes and my share of hospitalization, he concluded, "And of course we'll deduct a few pennies for FICA!" We're a long way from "a few pennies" now, and I wonder how much workers in the year 2012 will have to pay to let me retire. By 2012 the United States will experience a massive population shift, and a minority of workers will have to support a majority of retired folks. How much must they pay? 20%? 40%? 60%? 80%?

Or will we even get a benefit? A January 1989 *Forbes* article, "Social Security: the Bottom Line," points out some startling realities about the system: A person who retired in 1988 at age 65 after working for 45 years and paying the maximum rate would have contributed $38,000 in Social Security taxes. If his benefit stayed flat at $838 a month, he would recoup his entire $38,000 contribution within four years. From that moment to the day he dies every Social Security check is pure profit!

Not bad, huh? Well let's take a look at what younger people can expect from their contributions. The following example from *Forbes* is a real eye opener! If a worker entered the work force at 22 in 1980 and paid the maximum tax throughout his career, in terms of 1980 dollars he will have paid the equivalent of $475,000 in Social Security taxes by the time he retires in 2023. With a benefit of $1,250 a month, it will take him 32 years to recoup the value of what he paid in. Even the healthiest of us are not likely to recoup what we've paid into the system—let alone enjoy any profits!

As dismal as that forecast is, unless things change, with the rising cost of homes, cars, and college most folks our age won't be able to afford to retire anyway. For most of us it will be work until we drop.

But, some of us will be able to retire at 55—maybe younger. How? By learning how to maximize the purchasing power of our current incomes and how to invest our money wisely. Only this way can we build sufficient wealth to support ourselves, with or without Social Security. The choice is yours—retire at 55 and or work until 80 or older. Which do you want to do?

You do have a choice. That's what this book is all about. As you read and do the activities described in this book, you will begin to realize just how many choices you really have. The book teaches you how to maximize the power of these choices. It gives you methods and a plan. The only thing you must supply is the belief in yourself that you can do it!

IF WE DID IT, ANYONE CAN

I've read a lot of success stories. Many of them have a common plot about a kid who had a special knack for business practically from birth. You know how they go . . . about the kid who successfully sold newspapers, Christmas cards, seeds, then as a young adult started or joined a business that became a great success, etc., etc.

I don't have a glamorous childhood story. I was an average kid from a middle class midwestern family. Like other kids, I struggled through high school, getting at best average grades. I wasn't a big star in sports, or an officer in clubs, or anything like that. I tried to make money in the usual kid things, but had little success. The only childhood job that I had for any length of time was working in a gas station pumping gas and doing oil changes.

I never thought of myself as anything other than an average or perhaps slightly less than average Joe. Negative feedback during my childhood gave me a good-sized inferiority complex that didn't finally get cured until my mid-twenties. The cure was obtained via heavy doses of positive thinking, which started somewhere in college through the interests of some kind teachers who directed me to self-help books. These books combined with practice helped me gain self-confidence. It was the strength of that early encouragement that started me on the road to success.

That's why I say, "If we can do it. So can you!"

WHAT THIS BOOK IS ABOUT

Over the years my family and I developed a wealth building strategy. It's a strategy based on our earned wages, because that's all we have to work with. We didn't and don't have an inheritance, rich parents, or lucky gambling streaks. We have built our wealth on wages earned working a 9:00 to 5:00 job and some other part-time jobs.

This book reveals the strategy that changed us from net spenders to net savers. It can do the same for you no matter how much you earn. I consider this book a financial primer, a saver's owner's manual. It will show you how to magnify your current income to gain financial security and independence.

The book can also help you create a plan for your retirement that will let you determine when, where, and how you will retire. It will help you to use Social Security to your best benefit, and will keep you from the worst thing I can imagine . . . poverty in old age.

The basics of financial planning and investing are included. My greatest wish, however, is to convince you that it is possible for you to become wealthy, that you will come to understand and accept the power that is in thought alone. It's a power that directs your energies to fulfillment of the goal—a power that will make you rich!

I want you to believe in yourself. You are an intelligent person capable of wisely handling your own money. Any mistakes you have made are not because you lack mathematical or business skills, but only because you lacked knowledge.

Accept the fact that the only financial advisor you need is yourself. Only *you* have a vested interest in your success. Only *you* can do what is necessary to achieve it.

I also want you to understand that there are no great mysteries to making money. You are capable of understanding all the tools that are available, including the financial pages of the newspaper, once you know the code.

Think about it. If knowledge is indeed power, at no point in our educational system do we teach students what they need to know to gain financial power. Kids need to learn the basics: How to balance a check book, how to do taxes, how to pay utilities, how to read and understand apartment leases, mortgages, and installment loan agreements, how to deal with lawyers, how to file simple legal documents, etc.

Until all high school students are required to take a course that covers all the basics for financial survival, how can they be expected to go out in the world and achieve great success?

We enter the work world financially ignorant. So you're not alone, and the war isn't lost. You've just begun and I'm going to give you the guns and ammunition to win!

CHAPTER **2**

Confessions of an Ex-Credit Card Junkie

Do I know how it is to be in debt? Over my head? Unable to make it from pay day to pay day without floating a personal check until I got the funds to cover it? You bet I know!

I was a credit card junkie. For about ten years of my life plastic and checks were the only currency I used. My life was an endless cycle of revolving charge and installment loan payments. I never paid off any loan. When I bought something like a new car, the balance of the old car loan was added to the new loan.

I fell so deep in debt that I could no longer live without credit cards. I had to use them exclusively because I had no savings, no cash reserves, no surplus left from my paycheck after I paid all my bills.

The interest and finance charges I paid during that period were disgraceful. I wish I could tell you the exact amounts, but when I finally cleared my debt I burned the statements in celebration. I can tell you, though, that almost 50% of my gross annual income went to pay credit card payments. In net terms, we're talking nearly 70% of my spendable income. When you add another 28% for a home mortgage and 7% more for a car loan, you can see how much in trouble I was.

I use the term "junkie" because as with drugs, once you become "hooked," it's nearly impossible to end your credit dependence until you take the cure. The best cure is to quit cold turkey. Revolving cards charge extraordinary rates of interest, ranging from 15% to 22%. Compare this to the 8.5% to 11% charged for secured loans like car loans. When you make installment payments on a credit card you're actually repaying borrowed money like you would for a secured loan. However, unlike a secured loan, you pay premiums of 50% to 100% more for the privilege. That's very expensive money!

Unless you pay off the balance each month (see Figure 2-1), the interest compounds. More purchases make matters worse until you come to the point where you are unable to pay any more than the minimum payment. You are up on a payment treadmill, running full speed and going nowhere. You're hooked.

I was caught in a maddening cycle of payments from which I could not escape. I had no savings so I couldn't take advantage of any special sales or bargains beyond my credit limit. Toward the end of this period of my life, it got so bad that I had to use cash advances from one card to make payments on my other cards.

I am not criticizing the use of credit cards nor the finance charges credit card companies assess. The reason they charge higher interest rates, after all, is that credit card debt carries higher risk of nonpayment. My comments are directed toward credit card abuse, because I am critically aware of how easy it is to misuse credit and to get into trouble when you are as naive and ignorant of finances as I used to be.

JUST 48 EASY PAYMENTS . . .

"Don't bother me with the details . . . just tell me what my payments will be!" I shudder when I recall those words. For me the measure of affordability was whether or not I could afford the payment. It didn't matter to me how much the interest rate was or how long the term of the loan was. All that was important

Figure 2-1: Paying for the Privilege

This chart demonstrates how credit card charges can compound when only minimum payments are made. These charts provide useful insight into how easily it is to become trapped by abusive credit card practices.
     Note the huge percentage of interest paid starting at 36 months. Compare this with the interest paid during the first year in both tables.

Table A
$1,200 balance @ 18.2% per annum finance charge
(minimum payment schedule)

Time Period	Monthly Payment Range	Interest per Year	Interest Paid as % of Amt. Charged	Balance Remaining
12 mos	$42.00–33.69	$195.99	20.4%	$962.60
24 mos	$33.02–26.49	$350.09	29.2%	$756.85
36 mos	$25.96–20.83	$471.25	39.3%	$595.08
48 mos	$20.41–16.38	$566.51	47.2%	$467.88
60 mos	$16.05–12.88	$641.41	53.5%	$367.88

Table B
$5,000 balance @ 21.8% per annum finance charge
(minimum payment schedule)

Time Period	Monthly Payment Range	Interest per Year	Interest Paid as % of Amt. Charged	Balance Remaining
12 mos	$175.00–145.18	$ 994.14	19.9%	$4,147.98
24 mos	$142.73–118.41	$1,804.98	36.0%	$3,383.19
36 mos	$116.42–96.58	$2,466.32	49.3%	$2,759.42
48 mos	$ 94.95–78.77	$3,005.73	60.0%	$2,250.65
60 mos	$ 77.45–64.25	$3,445.69	69.0%	$1,835.68

Credit card companies calculate the per annum finance charge as a percentage of the average monthly balance not the original amount charged shown here. The percentage shown represents actual cash paid compared to the amount of the original credit balance.

to me was having what I wanted when I wanted it. Pretty bizarre, huh? Or is it?

How many times have you convinced yourself that you just had to have the object of your desire even though your conscience was telling you that it cost too much. How many times did you finally justify the purchase with comments like, "Yes, but don't I deserve it? I should have something to show for all my hard work."

Developing a "payment mentality" is a dangerous thing. It takes the reality of cost, value, and affordability out of your purchase decisions. It reduces you to nothing more than a consumer. Your life and money become devoted to endless consumption. You have dedicated yourself to having things instead of becoming wealthy.

LOTS OF CHECKS, NO BALANCE

In those days I also was a great user of checks (and of course the two checking accounts I used had monthly service charges). Check writing is a great mind game. Somehow writing a check for $10.00 eight to ten times a week is less painful than writing one big check. Writing little checks lets you avoid the anguish of estimating how much you really need for the week—and the distress of living within the estimate.

I used to claim that I wrote so many checks because I was worried about carrying a lot of cash around. The truth was that it was easier for me to blow little parcels of money on wasteful things knowing that I still had some money left in my account. I never planned my purchases. I just went merrily along cashing little checks until my balance was zero. In this way I deferred worry until I spent my last penny.

But the system was flawed. If you write dozens of checks each month, balancing your checkbook is a nightmare. My solution was to balance my checkbook only when necessary.

Most of the time that meant only after checks started to bounce.

If you think about it, constant check writing and the payment mentality have a lot in common. In both circumstances you are not concerned about anything other than one small transaction or payment. You defer worry until you must cough up real money. Both are ways of deceiving yourself into believing you are not really that bad off.

A NEW TWIST ON OLD BEHAVIOR

What's the psychology behind this kind of behavior? An article entitled "Money Matters of the Mind" in *U.S. News & World Report* identifies it as heeding only one's "visual reality." In other words, seeing is believing. New York psychologist Georgia Witkin says, "Human beings evolved depending on visual reality. With credit cards, you can't see the money go, so it isn't real." I believe the same can hold true for checks.

Let's consider two of the latest "money substitutes" —automated teller machines and credit card checks. I thank God neither of these was around when I was a credit card junkie or I might not have ever escaped.

ATMs and credit card checks used properly are wonderful tools. Used improperly, both are even more dangerous than credit cards and checking accounts because of the speed at which they deliver service, their expanded accessibility, and their addictive qualities.

ATMs are giant Skinner boxes[1]. You insert your card. Type in an appropriate code and bingo! You're rewarded with

---

[1] *Skinner boxes were devices psychologist William B. Skinner used to study animal behavior. They were boxes with two paddles. Pigeons were trained to press one paddle in preference to another to get a food reward. This conditioning or behavior modification applies to humans as well as pigeons.*

cash any time you want it, 24 hours a day. Friends of mine tell me they use these machines all the time just like I used checks. They tell me that the problem with ATMs is that they run out of cash much faster than when they use their checking accounts exclusively.

That's where the second new "cash substitute" may come into play. It's a natural extension of the ATM. If you run out of cash you can write yourself a loan with one of the new credit card checks. Immediately you have instant access to any amount of cash (over $150) up to your credit limit. The card is accepted any time of day or night anywhere. But as soon as you cash the check your finance charges start.

The purpose of this book is not a discourse on the psychology of human spending. It is to teach you how to become rich. But you can do this only if you are aware of all the factors that can impede your progress—including those going on in your own mind.

More detail on this and other "poverty-oriented" behavior is provided in Chapter Six on budgeting, but for now prove it to yourself. Try to observe what kind of people prefer to use checks, credit cards, ATM's, and credit card checks rather than cash. Compare them with the types who mostly use cash. Pay particular attention to those who use credit cards and checks to buy things that cost less than $20.

With some exceptions, middle and lower income groups are the biggest check-writers and card-users. I also believe the same type of people are the biggest users of ATMs and credit card checks. For everyday purchases, rich folks usually use more cash. This is particularly true when there is a discount for using cash, as for gasoline purchases.

If I've been describing you, don't despair. I was there, too! Debtors prison doesn't exist. You aren't sentenced to a life-time of debt and poverty. Things can and will change.

I said that I had never saved a nickel. This is not quite accurate. I did save. However, what savings I did were spending oriented. For example, I participated in bank Christmas Clubs (a great gimmick). It worked like this: The bank gave you a payment book that would allow you to save the amount you desired for spending on Christmas gifts the following year. You didn't earn a dime of interest, but that wasn't your goal anyway. You saved only to spend, spend, spend bigger next year. This is slightly better behavior than using credit cards, but it's still consumption oriented and can never help you become wealthy.

I was also a big saver of trading stamps. This meant I usually spent more by shopping at the stores that gave me trading stamps. At redemption time the situation reversed. The actual cash value of the stamps I redeemed was worth less in merchandise than what I paid to get them.

I still have a half dozen worthless books of stamps that never got redeemed, because I didn't have enough to get anything worthwhile. Ironic, huh? Waiting to get something of greater value resulted in getting nothing. In my mind this is a perfect example of where consuming behavior will take you.

TWO DISASTERS = AN OPPORTUNITY

By the time I turned 32, I was on the verge of financial catastrophe. All the symptoms were there. No matter how much money I made, there never was enough. I was taking cash advances on my bankcard to pay other debts. Checks were bouncing, payments were late, things were wearing out, and I couldn't replace them for lack of money or even credit.

I had two basic choices: Sell my assets to clear my debts or file personal bankruptcy. I examined bankruptcy but chose to pay off my debts instead. I feel bankruptcy is an act of desperation and should be used only if you have no assets. Bankruptcy literally means that those who lent you money in good faith will not be paid. If I lent someone money in good faith, I would hope they would pay me back unless it was impossible. So for me, bankruptcy was too harsh an alternative.

Instead I decided to sell the house and use the equity to pay off all my debts. Fortunately there was enough, with a few thousand left over. Why didn't I take a mortgage equity loan? First, that option wasn't available to me, for various reasons, and, second, if it had been, it wouldn't have solved my problem. The debt would have remained, and the payments. Having cleared my credit card balances, I probably would have gone right back to spending.

Did I change my ways? Not entirely. I cut up all my cards except American Express, because I used it for business. Also at that time the card offered no revolving credit so I had to pay the balance, on time, at the end of each month.

I spent $2,000 of my proceeds on what I regarded were essentials: a new stereo, a new mattress set, and a couple of decorator chairs. I was left with about $2,000 in savings.

My new life was debt-free. It felt marvelous. But I still spent every cent I made. A couple of years later I married the love of my life. She's a wonderful lady, and a much better saver. She had saved over $6,000. So we started our married life with $8,000—more money than I had ever seen before!

We enjoyed a year of happy Yuppydom spending every nickel I made. Oh, the joys of spending without debt! I felt secure, because for the first time in my life I had money for that proverbial rainy day. Little did I know how close that day was!

Learning the Hard Way: The Lessons
My Depression-Era Parents Tried in Vain To Teach Me

My day of reckoning came the next year. I was working for a large consumer magazine selling advertising space. For my age and level of experience I was doing very well. At 35, I was making $38,000 per year ($60,000 in 1990 dollars). I had a company car, a nice expense account, a big office, and travel perks. My boss was demanding, but given the pressures of the business understandably so.

But I felt I was too good for what I was doing. One day in a moment of anger I quit. I was confident that I could easily find a better job than the one I had. After all, several jobs had been offered to me the previous year. I was confident in my abilities. I was also terribly ignorant of the financial realities of 1981. The United States had been in one of the worst recessions in recent times. People were being laid off in large numbers and brilliant me let my pride drive me from relative wealth and comfort to instant poverty in one easy step.

From Big Money to Instant Poverty in Ten Seconds

Since I quit my job I didn't qualify for unemployment compensation. I wasn't worried, though. I had confidence in my abilities and $8,000 in the bank, plenty to finance the few short weeks it would take to land another job.

With the job also went my company car, something in haste I had forgotten to figure in. No problem. I'd just buy another car. I planned on buying some new spiffy little job that was good on gas, had a good warranty, and so forth. I would be stepping down from my full-sized company car, but I could handle it. Unfortunately, having no job meant no credit for a car. I would have to pay cash if I wanted a new car.

That jarred me! Paying cash for a car would take a big chunk out of our nest egg. But I had some strong job leads, including a final interview with another consumer magazine. So I decided to hold off on my car purchase for a few days pending the final interview.

It happened to be Thanksgiving weekend. This was a particularly depressing holiday. Vic, our son, was barely a month old and needed everything. My wife had a difficult and costly pregnancy. We didn't have health insurance coverage and were paying cash installments to the hospital and doctor. The baby didn't have any of the little niceties. In fact, he didn't have even necessities like winter clothing.

So there I was on Thanksgiving Day: Out of work, no car, shrinking funds, medical bills, and a month-old baby. And over our objections, our landlord had made the decision for us that since we had a baby we would have to rent a two-bedroom apartment. He wouldn't renew our lease unless we complied. We didn't like the fact that we had no choice in the matter so we had agreed to move. So added to our misery was moving to a new apartment in December, no joy if you consider the weather in Chicago.

Somehow I knew we'd make it through all these difficulties in the couple of weeks it would take until I'd return to the comfort of the advertising business. I decided to take a mid-day walk to help me think things through and relieve my anxieties.

It was a bright, sunny, cold Thanksgiving day. As I walked down the street a family drove by in an old Chevy. They looked so warm and comfortable. Chilled by the wintry November air I thought, "How lucky those people are to have that car!" I caught myself in mid-thought. Before that day I would have thought how unlucky those poor folks were to have to drive an ugly, rusting, old Chevy!

That thought gave birth to the new me. In one moment I realized how privileged my life had been up to that point, how I took so many things for granted, expected luxuries not necessities. I nearly wept. It was an important change, one that would eventually lead me to the road to wealth.

The following Monday we bought a like-new diesel Rabbit for $5,000, leaving us with about $2,500 for the month or so it would take me to find a new job. I didn't get the one job that had been promised to me because the manager who planned to hire me was demoted and had to take the job himself. My other leads also turned cold.

I suddenly became overqualified. Nobody would hire me even for a lesser job. I was told that I wouldn't be happy and would end up quitting. There were very few jobs and hundreds of applicants. I became discouraged and depressed as the time went on.

One month turned into ten months. The $2,500 disappeared and we had to go into debt to survive. My wife's wonderful older brother helped us with monthly checks that paid the groceries and rent. No jobs were in sight, especially for advertising types. During recessions the first budgets that get cut are advertising budgets. No budgets means there is no money to buy ad pages and no need for advertising salesmen to sell them—no need even for salesmen with great sales records.

We prayed, we hoped, and I searched. I read and reread my positive thinking books. A line in one book almost brought me to the point of rage. It said something like "sometimes opportunity is disguised in misfortune or temporary setbacks." I didn't realize until many years later how prophetic those lines were. At the time they just seemed to underscore my misery.

I am lucky and blessed, though. Blessed to have an understanding, compassionate wife who never lost faith in me. She would assure me that everything would turn out all right. She made an adventure out of our circumstances. For example, she decided that we would eat only things that were on sale and preferably those items on the bruised, dented, and past freshness date displays.

Toughing It Out

One week potatoes were 89¢ for ten pounds. We bought two bags and made it our goal to figure out different ways to serve them for a week. Yes, we supplemented some dinners with cheap cuts of meat, but essentially we ate potatoes for the entire week. We came up with some pretty interesting things:

Potato soup, potato pancakes, potato casseroles, and much more. You'd be surprised how creative you can be when you want to, even in times of distress.

We invented the slogan, *"It's not for sale unless it's on sale!"* and made it our motto. Vic was raised on it and today proudly recites it whenever we go shopping.

In between job interviews we spent time together on shopping tours and in the library. The shopping tours were for looking only—it was about the only leisure activity we could afford. The Rabbit gave us 50 miles per gallon, which meant we could spend a whole day exploring for less than $2 worth of fuel. We searched for bargains. We learned how to make deals, find treasures in closeouts, rebates, and coupons. We learned the prices for every household item from pea soup to oriental carpets.

The library helped me fill the hours. At first I went to search the want ads and look up the addresses of publishers and agencies to write job inquiry letters to. After several months I began to run out of leads. Depression drove me into temporary retreat. For the next few weeks I exercised, watched TV, played with the baby, made some telephone calls, and pretended not to be out of work. Inactivity and fear started to get to me. So I asked my wife if she thought it would be a good idea for me to spend time in the library researching things I didn't know anything about. Two things came immediately to mind: economics and investing.

I had always been intrigued with the prospect of hitting it big in the stock market. Although I didn't have the slightest idea of how to do that, I knew if I just could get a couple of bucks together and get the right tips I could pull it off. Thank God I never had enough money! As I soon learned, getting the right tips is a sucker's play, sure to lose money, as I will explain later on in this book.

I spent six months in intensive research and by the time I went back to work, I could talk with understanding to any investor or broker. I was ready to give my new-found skills a try. I only lacked one thing. Money.

A FRESH START

Our trial ended nearly a year after it had begun. Through the help of a friend, I got a job in ad sales with a publisher's rep—at two thirds of my previous earnings. I was glad to have the job no matter what it paid. Income aside, I started this job with something I never had before: goals.

My first goal was to pay back my wife for her patience, love, and support. Despite her protests, I knew that a house in the suburbs was something she really wanted. I was in debt and had no idea how I could scrape together enough to pay off my debts, let alone save a sizeable down payment. Nonetheless, I felt I owed her for her loving support. Somehow I would do it.

My second goal was to learn to swallow my pride, do the best I knew how, and hang on to this new job. Tied to this was my third goal: a desire to own my own business. I felt that only by owning my own business would I ever be free from the tyrannies of office and management politics.

All three goals had a common root. They all required considerable sums of money, and money was something I didn't have. Or did I? During my unemployment I had abundant time to think. I realized then that I didn't have an exact handle on how much or on what kind of things I spent my money. Oh, I knew approximately what I had spent yesterday, but not precisely how much or on what it was spent.

Keeping Track of Our Progress

We began to record daily every penny we spent. At first we used a small notebook. Later we advanced to ledger paper.

Regardless of what we used, we recorded our expenditures faithfully.

At the end of each month we totalled our expenses by category: food, eating out, commuting, household expenses, utilities, other. We soon discovered pockets of waste. A few too many meals out, fluctuating electric and telephone bills, fuel bills that were too high in one month versus another, goodies that should have been bought in volume, etc. In fact, through some smart shopping we found that we could save 20% of my net paycheck. This grew to 40% as we became more skilled.

Before the year was out, we had cleared our debts and had begun saving for our house. I wish I could say that it all went happily ever after from that point, but it didn't. Shortly after starting my new job, it was jeopardized by the loss of a major account. This was not just any major account; it happened to be the account of the friend who had recommended me for the job. Complicating matters, he decided to hire my office manager to work on his own staff.

I was left on very shaky ground. Since I was a friend of this client, the rep had probably hired me feeling that he was securing the account. In fact, he not only lost the account, but also an employee he valued.

The rep was kind in his dealings with me but offered no assurances about whether or not the office was staying open. After nearly a year of unemployment I was scared. Frantically I tried to replace the account but realized that it might take more time than my boss was willing to allow. When another job became available, I grabbed it.

Hanging on to this job was even tougher. I was forced to travel 80% of the time, which was hard on my family, and I worked for an organization that knew only one way of doing business . . . their way. Being on straight commission I found this to be intolerable because they weren't always right. Scared to lose the job but miserable in it I decided I would do everything to keep it.

OUT OF WORK AGAIN—BUT SMARTER

We scrimped and saved and in two years we had nearly saved back our original nest egg of $8,000. Then disaster struck! Politics overpowered performance; I was fired. Luckily this time I was entitled to vacation pay, unemployment compensation, and earned commissions.

I felt like I had been hit over the head with a hammer, but I was in much better shape this time to handle it. It didn't stop me from breaking down and sobbing at the unemployment window. An understanding, white haired clerk reassured me kindly and helped me prepare the necessary forms. She made me feel good. I wish I knew her name. I'd like to thank her for her kindness.

Running Our Household Like a Business

A couple of months later I landed a good job paying about the same as the job I had quit three years before. I decided that the time was right to formalize our guerilla savings program. I also decided to try something very different.

Many years before, I had heard a lecturer state that most successful corporate businesspeople will fail at the only business they will ever own—their own household. The idea of my household being really a business had intrigued me, but I never did anything about it. Now I was willing to try anything to succeed. So I decided that if my household really is a business why not run it like one, with a strategic plan, an annual budget, and balance sheets. We would buy like a business. Invest like a business. *Be* a business!

Each month we would do balance sheets to determine our savings. We would operate on a calendar fiscal year and have an annual Board of Directors meeting to prepare a formal budget. Each of us would also assume a role. My wife would be

Executive Vice President for Purchasing. All purchases would be negotiated by her, or at least through her. It was and is her job to make purchasing a refined art. I would be Director of Finance. It would be up to me to pay all the bills, keep the necessary records, and handle the investing. Vic was too little for an assignment, but he will be given one as soon as we feel he is ready.

To keep us on track with the goals of owning a house and having a business we decided to establish a five year plan. The plan would list our yearly savings and investment goals.

At first I felt that committing to a goal five years in advance was unrealistic, but I went along with the idea rationalizing that having even an unlikely target was better than having no target at all. I smiled as I wrote down what I thought was absurd: I declared that we would have a net worth of $100,000 by five years hence. With only $10,000 saved I thought the goal was ridiculous, but I wrote it down anyway.

FROM DEBT TO SUBSTANTIAL EQUITY

We reached our five-year goal in less than three years. By the time eight years had passed from the time I quit my job, we had attained a net worth exceeding $350,000. We had amassed this amount basically from salary income ranging from $24,000 to $50,000.

Did we save it all? Of course not! We saved enough to use to grow more money. We saved a cash horde from which we made wise investments in real estate, the stock and bond markets, gems, and valuables. These investments doubled and tripled in value. We saved, bought, and sold.

Did we take some extraordinary measures to save? You bet! But, the methods we used were not illegal, immoral, or even risky. We still use them. All they required is desire, discipline, and the daring to try something unconventional. In short, guts!

I have interviewed several self-made millionaires and without exception they all are willing to do things differently. They care little about what others think. They are goal-directed and very conservative spenders. They are without a doubt a gutsy group, and I say this with great respect!

My family and I plan on joining them. There's room for you too! Enough of the past: It's time for the future—your future as a wealthy person. You are ready to begin. Keep an open mind and the resolve to succeed. Let's go!

CHAPTER 3

Getting Started: Knowing Your Financial Situation

How much did you spend last week? How about yesterday? Central to any wealth-building strategy is knowing precisely how you spend your money. Approximations are no good, because they fail to consider the literally hundreds of small items you buy each month. These items, though of little importance one by one, in total offer substantial pockets of saving.

This is one of the first things I discovered after I began logging our expenses. Before then I didn't have the vaguest idea where our money went. Although I was disturbed by my discoveries, I was also exhilarated by the thought that I might be onto something that could really help us.

One discovery, at first, seemed very trivial. Every day without fail I bought two large cups of coffee from the convenience store near the train station. Each cup of coffee cost 65¢ plus tax for a daily total of $1.39. Some days I also bought a 65¢ roll. The monthly total for these items alone was $33 or nearly $400 a year, not counting lost interest. My wife reasoned that we could do some painless savings if I took my coffee from home instead of buying it at the convenience store. So she bought me a supply of styrofoam cups and faithfully made me two cups of coffee to carry to the train every morning. My coffee costs fell to less than $2 a week for a net savings of $25 per month. Later we discovered we could save an additional $1 or more by washing and reusing the cups. More about this later in Chapter Four on guerilla savings.

We found that each week I spent even more on gum, candy bars, and soft drinks from the newsstand in the building. Like my morning coffee, I still could have these things if I brought them from home. Between my coffee and daily incidentals I could save over $50 a month—$651 a year at a minimal rate of interest. We could save money without sacrifice, other than a little time and effort. What a discovery!

We searched for more pockets of waste and uncovered many. One was my lunches. Because I was in advertising, many of my meals were spent with clients and consequently were paid for by my expense account. That's probably why I didn't pay much attention to the lunches I paid for myself.

Our expense logs indicated that, on the average, I ate three lunches a week at my own expense. These lunches had an average cost $5.50 including tip or $66 a month, $792 a year. My wife would make me a more nutritious and healthy lunch for less than a third of that, netting us an additional $528 in savings.

Before that time I was also a fanatic about sending my clothes to the cleaners. White shirts had to be cleaned and starched to military standards. Suits went to the cleaners faithfully after two wearings. My cleaning bills were outrageous!

We easily cut our cleaning costs by two-thirds. We soon realized a secondary benefit . . . my clothes lasted longer. I had no idea that excessive cleaning faded suits, and commercial laundering and starching frayed and yellowed my shirts in a relatively short time. Reducing my cleaning bills saved us nearly $700 a year, and the extended life of my shirts and suits also allowed us to reduce clothing purchases by one suit and a half dozen or so shirts a year. Total savings: More than $1,000 a year!

So by analyzing three small, almost unconscious frequent purchases, we were able to save more than $2,000 a year, including interest. All were the result of discoveries we made after we began tracking our expenses. Once you start tracking your expenses you will never again lose money on small things.

Remember hundreds of tiny holes can sink a ship just as easily as one big hole.

CHARTING YOUR COURSE

On the following pages I have provided some tracking tools to help you get started on your own program. The first two in Figures 3-1 and 3-2, "Retail Treasure Locator" and "Convenience Treasure Locator," are designed to help you speed the process of finding your pockets of wealth. They give you a quick assessment of how you are doing.

You may be tempted to cheat. Resist! These tools are for discovery only, not for criticism. It was only after I started to fess up to the error of my ways that I was able to start building my wealth. It has been said that confession is good for the soul. I'm here to tell you that it's good for your pocketbook as well!

I suggest that you do these activities when no one is around—especially your friends. That way you avoid any possible criticism at this early stage when you are particularly vulnerable. (The need for secrecy will be discussed more fully later in this chapter.) Also do the activity when you have time to think; wait until the kids go to bed or to school.

Figure 3-3 on page 35 is our Expense Diary. If you are an accountant or a bookkeeper, you may snicker at its design. If you do make a better one for yourself, send me a copy. I'm always looking for ways to improve.

I sketched out some general categories I thought would be appropriate for most family uses. You are welcome to copy this form or make your own on ledger paper. The idea is to get you and your family into the daily habit of writing down all your expenses and categorizing them into some general accounts for analysis later.

You may also find it helpful to keep one main ledger in the house and have several small expense notebooks in strategic

Figure 3-1: Retail Treasure Locator

(A) *Items Purchased at Retail*	(B)	(C) *Price Paid x .60 = Sale Price*
1.		
2.		
3.		
4.		
5.		
6.		
7.		
8.		
9.		

Total (B) $_____ Total (C) $_____

Total (B) $_____
minus   Total (C) $_____
SAVINGS $_____

Instructions: Look at some items in your pantry or refrigerator that you purchased at the regular or retail price. Choose items $2 or more in price. Write the name of each item in column (A) and its price in column (B). Multiply each price in column (B) by .60 and enter your answer in column (C). The result is the sale or promotional price you could have paid.

Add all the items in (B) and enter the total in the spaces provided. Do the same for the prices in (C). Next subtract total (B) from (C) to determine the total savings you could have received.

Figure 3-2: Convenience Treasure Locator

(A) *Convenience Store Items*	(B) (C) *Price Paid x .50 = Sale Price*	
1.		
2.		
3.		
4.		
5.		
6.		
7.		
8.		
9.		

Total (B) $_____ Total (C) $_____

Total (B) $_____

minus   Total (C) $_____

SAVINGS $_____

Instructions: Look again at some items in your pantry or refrigerator that you purchased at a convenience store at their regular price. Usually these are common items that are frequently purchased like bread, milk, cigarettes, soft drinks, beer, or deli items, etc.

Again choose items $2 or more in price. Write the name of each item in column (A) and its price in column (B). This time multiply each price in column (B) by .50 and enter your answer in column (C). The result is the sale or promotional price you could have paid.

Add all the items in (B) and enter the total in the spaces provided. Do the same for the prices in (C). Next subtract total (B) from (C) to determine the total savings you could have received.

places like the glove compartment of the car or your purse or briefcase to record expenses as they occur. At the end of the day you can transfer your expenses to your main ledger.

How you do this is less important than just developing the discipline to record your expenses. If there are two of you, you have the advantage of reminding each other of your daily duty. Make it fun. Don't nag each other—at least, not yet!

Faithfully record your expenses daily for several months without changing your normal spending patterns. *This is important!* If you try to start cutting back on expenses right away you will temporarily lose track of small expenses that will come back to sabotage your budget later. So for two to three months simply record your expenses without making any changes in your spending patterns. You may want to lengthen the time frame to four or even six months to get a broader perspective. I don't think this is necessary. Three months is usually sufficient to help spot the small frequent money wasters.

After two to three months of logging expenses, go back and review them. Look for *painless* ways to save money like the kinds of things I have described already. Take a red pen and circle them. Try to find patterns or groupings of similar expenses. Locating a spending pattern is like finding a vein of rich ore.

As eager as you may be to get started, I suggest that you first center on savings that can be accomplished by easy adjustments. Like losing weight, crash diets and heavy exercising right from the start are not only torturous they are counterproductive!

Changing habits takes time. You must ease into change so that you will stay committed to your goal. Trying to do too much too soon will only frustrate you and tempt you to abandon your goal. You probably bought this book because you want to change your life. You want to enjoy financial freedom and financial security. This all can be yours, but you must be able to walk before you can run. Start by taking small first steps. Do

Figure 3-3: Expense Diary

Below is a sample diary with general expense categories labeled for you. We use six-column sheets because we find them easier to handle and less expensive to buy than larger ledger sheets. However, to make room for more expense categories and to distinguish figures on this smaller sheet, we use underlining and parentheses. If you find this confusing use a larger sheet with more columns and designate one expense category per column instead of two.

EXPENSE DIARY, MONTH of _____

	DATE PAID	EXPENSES ITEMIZED	1 PAYMENTS FIXED (UTILITIES)	2 FOOD GROCERIES (EAT-OUT)	3 TRANSPOR. FUEL/MAIN. (COM./TRAV)	4 HOME REPAIR/SUPPL (FURN/APPL)	5 FAMILY CLOTHING (MED/DEN)	6 MISC.
1		Mortgage/Rent						
2		Payment: Car						
3		Payment: _____						
4		Payment: _____						
5		Heat	( )					
6		Electricity	( )					
7		Telephone	( )					
8		Water	( )					
9		Garbage	( )					
10		↑						
11		Label						
12		each of						
13		your						
14		expenses						
15		as they						
16		occur						
17		in these						
18		rows						
19								
20		↓						
21								
22								
23								
24								
25								
26								
27								
28								
29		Total _____						
30		Total ( )	( )	( )	( )	( )	( )	

the first two activities and start your own Expense Diary. Read the rest of the book, but start your diary today!

(*A side note:* If you are deep in debt, don't despair! Remember I was there too. If you are in this position you may find it helpful to skip to Chapter Ten, "Solutions for Credit Kamikazes," after you finish this chapter. Then come back and continue reading the rest of the book.)

You will note that the title of this book is *Wealth on Your Paycheck.* There is no mention of the words "fast" or "easy." I don't want to delude you. The program described in this book works, as I know from firsthand experience, but this isn't a get-rich-quick scheme. I don't believe in them. I have made it my personal mission to discover what it takes to become rich starting with little or nothing. I have researched autobiographies of self-made millionaires, and I have also personally met several. Almost without exception, none have made their fortunes from get-rich-quick schemes.

Anyone who claims to have made a fortune quickly and easily I'm very cautious of. I'm even more cautious of those who try to persuade me into a get-rich-quick scheme. Most of the time these guys are fast talk operators looking for a mark, and the only one who will get rich quick is them.

The program described in this book takes time and effort. It works faster than you may think and is easier than you may believe. However, the factor that determines how fast it will work is the strength of your personal commitment. Make the pursuit of wealth your lifetime goal and you begin to see results almost immediately. Do it part time and it will take longer.

Regardless of how deeply committed you become, just using a few of the techniques and ideas reported in this book will improve your financial situation.

WHY THE RICH GET RICHER

While we're talking about rich folks we ought to examine their habits to determine how they get there and stay there. Like I've said already, the rich folks I'm most interested in are those who are self-made, folks who started out like you and me but through wits, luck, and timing made it to the ranks of the financially elite. They are living proof that it is still possible to become wealthy in America today.

Why do the rich get richer? I maintain that the answer is very simple and for the most part it is for reasons that most average folks wouldn't even think about: The rich get richer because they are far more careful with their money than other folks are!

At first, you may find this very hard to accept. I did. My first inclination was to believe that the rich get richer because they are pulling tricks on us innocents to take our money. I think this belief that the rich are a ruthless lot ready to pounce on us is very common in America. I've tried to analyze how we have come to believe this but can't identify any single source.

Perhaps it comes from news stories of some millionaire being indicted for tax evasion. Truth is, there are probably hundreds of middle-class tax evaders for every millionaire, but their petty larcenies are not as easy to catch; nor are they as newsworthy. In fact they might draw sympathy instead of disdain. Maybe the feelings result from the politicians who spew out Robin Hood schemes of taxing the rich to give to the poor. Unfortunately, if we believe them too much and let them have their way, eventually there will be no rich left to tax.

Wherever these ideas come from, they are basically false. Rich folks are more careful with their money than the rest of us. Period. They always seek the best deal in whatever they buy.

They invest their money wisely and follow their investments carefully. They are politically active and are among the first to write their Senators and Representatives when repressive taxes are proposed.

I've sat in their homes and observed their behavior. I've noticed that their financial conservatism extends to even the smallest items. For example, I enjoy an occasional cocktail. My middle-class friends always serve me the best brands. My millionaire friends usually serve the best only for business purposes, switching to house brands for social entertaining.

I've also observed that the best-quality products and the best sales can often be found in the wealthier neighborhoods. In the poorest neighborhoods you'll find the poorest quality and the highest prices. This seems counter to market reason until you think about it. Rich folks won't pay for poor quality. Nor will they pay high prices for ordinary items. Rich folks are value- rather than brand-conscious. Poor folks are not as discriminating. They tend to determine value in terms of familiar brands. Buying is more of an emotional experience.

Merchants know this and charge what the market will bear. The result is that poor folks become poorer and rich folks become richer.

Poor folks are also captured by images of wealth. They attempt to experience wealth by rich living. They surround themselves with what they believe are the symbols of wealth like luxury cars, furs, fancy clothes, etc. Rich folks have these things too, but they represent a much smaller percentage of their earnings or holdings. Where a Mercedes may be a prudent purchase for a millionaire, a new Chevy may be extravagant for a poor man. Poor folks fail to grasp this.

Seeking wealth images instead of adopting wealth-building behavior can only make you poorer. Changed behavior, however, can in time make you wealthy. Take a step closer today to your new life as a wealthy person by adopting a conservative spending attitude. Be like the rich folk: Look for the best deals, use coupons and rebates, shop for sales, study the financial pages, and do the many other things described in this book. For now start by just adopting the behavior.

I hope to prove to you in this book that much of who and what you are is determined by attitudes and behavior. Attitudes determine behavior and behavior determines results. So the first attitude you must adopt is simply belief that you can achieve your goal of becoming wealthy. A second equally important attitude is to value your own knowledge and opinions above those of your friends and relatives. *Becoming wealthy is not a group activity.* It requires extraordinary individual resolve and courage, because wealth rests on a developed ability to see opportunity that others can't see. Since others cannot see the value you will see, you will be able to buy things cheap and sell them at a higher price later.

As you develop a self-reliant attitude you will become what sociologist David Riesman calls an *inner-directed* person. This behavior allows you to make better decisions because peer pressure is eliminated. You rely on your own acquired knowledge of value. *Inner direction* allows you to escape money-losing herd behavior. It enables you to see market realities and avoid the trap of expert opinion, which is often wrong. It lets you buy gold for the price of tin.

Outer-directed people, by contrast, base their decisions on group standards of acceptance. If it is stylish to buy items at full retail, they will do so no matter how much it costs them personally. *Outer direction* is lemming-like behavior that stampedes people into poor money-management decisions. Acting on impulse and emotion they wait for the market to be up to buy and as a result pay the highest prices. Then at the slightest downturn they panic and sell at a loss the stock they paid too much for. They buy faddish products to impress each other, only to be caught on a treadmill of endless purchases dictated by changes in fashion. They act on the wisdom of collective opinion. They are almost guaranteed never to be rich.

Since the world is made up of predominantly outer-directed folks, you will find it helpful to keep your wealth-building activities secret. There are several reasons for this. First, there is a very human emotion of not wanting to be left behind. Your friends and family want you to succeed. But there is safety in numbers, and your departure reduces the size of their safe group. They fear you may forget about them. Another reason is human jealousy, which in essence asks, "Why should you get rich instead of me?"

But probably one of the foremost reasons for secrecy is to avoid unnecessary criticism. Not understanding or appreciating your commitment, these folks might label you as cheap and miserly rather than frugal and conservative.

How can you expect any other response? They have not reached your level of financial maturity. If they had, they would recognize their own wasteful practices. You are especially vulnerable to criticism during the first stages of your wealth-building activity. You are on new ground and may be a bit unsure of yourself. Criticism can sidetrack your efforts. Save yourself some grief: Keep your activities, plans, and goals to yourself.

As you become skilled, you will discover an interesting side benefit of keeping your activities secret. Since you have not disclosed your secret, the only thing your friends will see is the result of your activities. In time you will have more and higher quality things than you've ever had before. As they see you grow rich before their eyes, your friends and relatives will wonder where your new-found wealth has come from. They might ask if you inherited money, won a lottery, or received a promotion. They'll never guess that your new prosperity is based on your current income. You'll gain an image of wealth without trying. What an interesting contradiction! Earlier I said that pursuing wealth images will make you poorer. Here, by following conservative spending and saving practices, you become richer and automatically gain a wealth image as a bonus!

With this kind of wealth image you will be able to spend less on gifts, but the gifts you give will have a much greater impact, as the following story will illustrate.

THE GIFT WEDDING DRESS

My mother had a friend who we all thought was very rich. Why? Because she told us so. Apparently, during the Forties and Fifties this lady and her husband had owned a very swanky club. She delighted us with stories and photos of all the stars who had played in their club. We saw movies of her big house replete with all the luxuries you would expect from a person of her stature.

At the time my mother had met her, she had long been a widow and was living with a nephew in the same apartment complex as my folks. By day she worked as a salesperson in a fancy ladies clothier in a nearby lake shore suburb.

I always wondered why, if she was so rich, did she need to work. My mother told me it was only for something to do—besides, it really was none of our business.

My mother's friend was very kind and generous to my family and particularly to my younger sister. When my sister became engaged she announced that she would buy her wedding dress for her from her employer's exclusive store. I was flabbergasted! I knew how expensive wedding dresses were in regular department stores but in her store it was likely to cost two to three times more. Even if she used her employee discount and the dress was on sale, it would still cost thousands.

"Surely it must be a simple dress," I thought. I was wrong! The dress was floor-length French silk and lace. My sister was fitted and the result was gorgeous.

She had proven to me in this act of great generosity the immensity of her wealth! I was a believer!

I sustained this belief for many years. My illusion was shattered a few years ago when she confided that the dress had remained unsold in the store for many years. Several women had tried it on but no one wanted to buy it. Like Cinderella's slipper it was meant for only one—my sister. She told me with a laugh that the owner of the store let her buy that dress for 25 bucks just to get rid of it!

Was the dress worth thousands? Yes and no. Definitely it had a perceived value worth thousands; it also had a replacement value worth thousands. However, knowing what she paid for it cheapened its value in my eyes and reduced the importance of the gift to me. Had she kept her mouth shut I would have maintained my perceptions to this day. But I would also have been denied a wonderful lesson in thrift.

The moral to this story is for you to develop a sensitivity for value and an understanding of human nature. Keep your plans, goals, and methods secret. Bask in the sunshine of your good fortune and be thankful. This behavior will enable you to capitalize on bargain bonanzas that will gain the respect of your peers and catapult you into riches you cannot now imagine.

THE RIGHT ATTITUDE

Recently I overheard a couple of women reviewing the grocery store sale pages in the newspaper. Their comments went something like this:

"Sarah, look, the large-size orange juice is on sale for $1.49 at Favors!" "That's a very good price, Ann, but look, plums, grapes, and bananas are on sale at the Quickmart." "Yeah . . . and steaks are $2.49 lb at Ruby's."

"You know, Sarah, those prices are great, but who has the time to run to three or four supermarkets?" "Yeah, Ann, I know its ridiculous!"

The only thing ridiculous about this conversation was how easily they dismissed saving money. Time is money. Their lack of willingness to spend a little time will cost them money, the most precious kind: Net after-tax money. I wondered how they would better use their time.

The point is to develop the attitude that you will make it your personal mission to find ways to stretch your income. Remember the two Treasure Locator exercises (Figures 3-1 and 3-2)? Take the time. It will pay!

I hear a lot of rationalizations like "Oh well, you gotta live!" Or "Everyone's entitled to have a little fun!" These innocent-sounding truisms are hard to argue with. They make you feel entitled to spend money even if you are spending it foolishly or plunging yourself dangerously into debt.

Divorce the thought that enjoyment of life and spending money are the same thing. Buying something may bring you momentary pleasure, but no material thing will ever bring you joy in life. Joy in life comes from within. It comes from a deep appreciation of everything you have, starting with life itself.

Instead develop the attitude that if you have to rationalize a purchase, you probably shouldn't make it. When you rationalize, you are arguing with your subconscious thought, which knows what's in your best interest no matter how emotional you are about the purchase.

Wild spending sprees have psychological roots far beyond the scope of this book but nonetheless important to note. Spending can be an escape like alcoholism, binge eating, or drug abuse. Ask an alcoholic why he drinks, he'll give you marvelous excuses. Or ask dieters why they are eating a 3,000-calorie lunch. Again you'll hear wonderful rationalizations.

Ending any addiction or bad habit starts by stopping the behavior. Adopt the attitude that you will not buy anything ever again without considering it carefully.

I also want to alter the way you view pocket change. I want you to gain a new respect for the lowly dime, nickel, even penny. In my credit card junkie days a favorite line of mine was, "Oh, it's just a dime." I literally threw change away: If it fell on the floor I wouldn't bother picking it up. If the change from a dollar amounted to a few pennies I'd leave them on the counter. And, heaven help me, I'd never lower myself to pick up a penny from the ground!

Great attitude, huh? Well, during my unemployment research days I was shocked to find out that the net after-tax profit margins for many major U.S. corporations clustered around the 2% to 3% level. Major institutional investors like big insurance companies were happy to get a 7% to 10% return on their portfolios. If you translate this into dollars, these high-level financial entities were earning only 2¢ to 10¢ profit on every dollar.

When I wasted nickels and dimes I was wasting a sum equal to the annual profits per dollar of every major corporation and institutional investor in the United States. That thought certainly elevates lowly pocket change to a more lofty status.

After discovering this I gained new respect for pocket change. To help me hang on to this respect, I decided to view pocket change as a percentage of a dollar rather than a denomination of a coin. Hence a nickel is 5% of a dollar, three cents are 3%, a quarter is 25% and so forth. I suggest that you try this. In the game of wealth building, every penny counts!

In conclusion, the road to new-found wealth begins by assessing your present situation. Knowing where your money goes is the first step in effective budgeting. Next you must change your attitudes about money and spending. You must discard spending rationalizations. You must be willing to invest your time and have a healthy respect for all money including the lowly penny.

The next step is a serious savings program I call *guerilla savings.* By earnest application of the principles presented in Chapter Four you can be well on the road to saving 40% or more of your net earnings.

CHAPTER **4**

Washing Ziploc® Bags: A Guide to Guerilla Savings

Ridiculous! This is how you may feel when you read some of the suggestions I make in the next few chapters. Yes, I agree that washing Ziploc® bags may seem bizarre—until you understand the philosophy behind it[1]. Ziploc® bags, paper napkins, towels, foil, and the entire category of disposable or single-use products are designed for convenience. They are time savers.

Remember again the old saying, "time is money?" When you use convenience products you are exchanging money for time, the time it would take to do the job the old-fashioned way. If you have only your current income to make you wealthy, then the only way you can become rich is by finding ways to magnify it. An easy way I found to magnify my income is to *reverse the convenience process*. By eliminating convenience products and services I exchange my time and effort for cash.

I can hear the objection already: "With the kind of work I do, my time is really too valuable to mess around with these type of things! That's why I use a maid service, take my car to the automatic car wash, buy small items from the convenience mart. . . ." The answer is: If you can use time to earn more money than you will save, obviously then you should save time. If, however, the time you are saving will not earn anything, then it pays you to eliminate costly conveniences.

---

[1] *Yes I admit to washing Ziploc® bags!*

As you read the following pages you may find that you are already doing some of the things I have suggested. Great! You are already on the road to riches. However, to achieve ultimate success you must make a total commitment. That's why I use the term *guerilla savings*. This term describes a savings method that:

1. Is covert or secret;
2. Attacks points of weakness in purchasing and investing to get the best deals and make the greatest profits;
3. Uses warriors who are zealots, totally dedicated to success and ready to do whatever it takes to achieve their objective.

Become a *guerilla saver!* Join me in the war for riches. Make the commitment to succeed. Think of it as an adventure and have fun. You are on one of the most exciting and rewarding quests of your life!

As you progress, see if you can find other ways to save money, some that I don't mention or possibly even know about. If you do, drop me a line and tell me about them. Your success is encouraging to me.

CONVENIENCE IS EXPENSIVE

Seventy-five cents for a can of pop? Never! It's amazing how easy it is for us members of the "convenience generation" to drop three quarters into a pop machine for a cold drink. That's 75% of a dollar for an item that you can buy on sale by the case for 17¢ each. The cost of this convenience is 400% more than the price of the same item on sale! That's a huge premium to pay for a cold can of pop.

Select any item that is produced to be convenient or disposable and you'll realize the same thing. Take disposable diapers, for instance—a wonderful convenience for an unpleasant job! On sale a large box costs $8.99. If you figure the average tot requires 5 to 6 changes per day, a box lasts only about a week. In two years parents invest nearly $1,000 in diapers!

Ancient alchemists spent their entire lives unsuccessfully trying to turn lead to gold. Disposable diaper marketers have discovered how to turn biological waste into gold. (I guess you could say, they've found a potty of gold at the end of the rainbow!)

The example I gave was based upon buying the diapers on sale. If you are a true convenience freak and buy the diapers at retail, your total cost will be somewhere around $1,500.

Even if you spent $300 on buying and laundering cloth diapers (and that's a lot!), you're still way ahead by using them. If they were good enough for Mama they're good enough for us. They also are much better for the environment.

I mentioned in Chapter Two that I found I could save over $500 a year by bringing my lunch to work instead of eating out. Try it. Once you do you'll be as shocked as I am to see what people will pay for lunch items from the take-out counters. I've seen folks pay $3.50 to $4.00 for a salad that you could easily make for 75¢.

Before we leave this topic we should talk about the second cousin to convenience—impulse purchases. These are worse than just buying out of convenience. Reason? Because you had no intention of buying the item in the first place.

Grocery and discount department stores know this. That's why there are special displays at the checkouts designed to prompt impulse buying. Individual candy bars and gum are positioned at child level, making them easy to see and grab. Magazines and tabloid newspapers beg to be read as you stand in line with nothing to do. Combs, nail clippers, pens, small calculators, and all other Τ & Τ (trinkets and trash) come into your line of sight as you pass through the line. Impulse buying results in needless purchases that cost too much. Speaking of these things opens up another category of money wasters.

BLUE WATERS = MONEY DOWN THE DRAIN

Years ago a beer company used the slogan "From the Land of Sky Blue Waters" to describe the quality of water that went into its beer. Today sky-blue waters describe millions of U.S. household toilets.

Blue toilet water is definitely not essential for life. In fact, I believe if you regularly vacuum and clean your carpets, don't allow dishes to stand, take the garbage out, and in general keep a tidy house there is little need for the whole host of room and carpet sprays and deodorizers. Yes, everybody needs a disinfectant spray or liquid once in a while, but I find it hard to comprehend our national obsession with odor.

Odor Overkill

In addition to using heavily scented laundry detergents, almost unconsciously we throw sweet-smelling strips into the dryer for a promised fresh smell. We hang freshener strips in our cars, slap odor-eating insoles into our shoes, fill our clothing drawers with sacks of fragrant sachets, and own armies of perfumes, body lotions, and colognes. Some of us have gone off the deep end with these kinds of products.

Besides odor masking products, there is an entire category of wipes, scrubbing agents, single application spray cleaners, and polishes that can be easily replaced with less sophisticated and cheaper cleaning agents. Similarly the entire health and beauty aids group is filled with nonessentials.

No, I'm not talking about giving up toothpaste, deodorant, makeup, shampoo, or hair-spray. What I *am* asking is why do you need a special conditioner, shampoo, and deodorant for each member of the family?

Do It Yourself

Shopping services, lawn services, painters, decorators, baby sitters . . . it's no wonder we've become a service economy. Everywhere you look there's another service to replace something our parents and grandparents did for themselves.

A couple of years ago I too caught a slight case of the disease. The eaves, gutters, and downspouts of that house we bought needed a good scraping, sanding, and painting. It was the kind of job I loathe. I called some cheap painters in for an estimate! Despite my best negotiating skills they would do the job for no less than $1,000 plus paint! The house was a small two-bedroom; I calculated that I could do the entire job in a couple of weekends.

It took me only 30 hours in total to do a first-class job. That's over $33 per hour. I still don't like painting, sanding, and scraping, but I'm $1,000 richer for doing it!

Look around your home. What services are you paying for that you could do yourself? Kids in my neighborhood get $8 to $10 dollars to mow an average lawn and $2 to $3 dollars an hour to baby sit. Do the lawn yourself and form a baby sitting bank where you and your friends make deposits and withdrawals of baby sitting time by watching each other's kids.

The Price of Fear

Many dollars are lost to fear products—bottled water, U.V. blocker sunglasses, radon detectors, organic fruits and vegetables. We've become obsessed with protecting ourselves whether we need to or not. Supermarkets in my area sell gallons upon gallons of bottled water. I am sure that the water is the highest quality, but I'm equally confident in the purity of our tap water.

I believe the fault lies with our instant access to information. It has unintentionally victimized us by allowing us to see too much data too quickly. We see some hapless folks across the country with polluted water supplies and we assume ours must be polluted also. This is backed up by reports in the next moment that some homes have dangerous radiation levels. Again we assume ours might have the same problem.

If you are concerned, check them out with your city or county officials. If that doesn't satisfy you, then have your water or house tested by a legitimate laboratory. But don't just buy products because you are afraid of an unknown danger. The danger may not exist, and you may end up paying hundreds or thousands of hard-earned dollars out of ignorance.

Be smart. Cut back on money-wasting nonessentials. Nonessentials are very expensive, because they are readily consumed and must be frequently replaced. Next time you shop, isolate these items in your grocery basket. Before you check out add up how much you're planning to spend on these things that you can really live without. Then bite the bullet. Tell the cashier you don't want them.

WASHING ZIPLOC® BAGS

But don't stop with nonessentials; examine all your expenditures. Search out any items that you buy out of convenience or impulse. Replace them with things you can buy on sale or make. You'll pay yourself for the effort.

Recycle products that you would normally discard after a single use. Ziploc® bags are a very good example. They are extremely durable and will hold up to many uses. We get eight to ten uses per bag before they are worn out.

Same goes for aluminum foil: It can be washed and reused. We've had the same roll of foil for the past five years. You're right if you thought that it's impossible to extend a single roll for five years just by washing and reusing sheets. The way to extend use is by using non-disposable substitutes like pots with lids, bowls with covers, even a bowl covered with a plate will work. Your refrigerator might not look neat, but the object is to save money, not win Donna Reed housekeeping contests!

You must unlearn automatic, wasteful behaviors. Who ever said that the best way to bake a turkey is in foil? It was the aluminum foil manufacturers who promoted roasting turkeys in foil during the Fifties. Get yourself a roasting pan from garage sales or flea markets. It does a better job and is reusable.

Never buy a garbage bag again! Every grocery store puts your weekly groceries into a wide assortment of great garbage bags: Plastic and paper. Won't hold all your trash? C'mon folks! Use two or three smaller bags and don't stuff them to overflowing!

Inconvenient? Yep—but look at the price you pay every week or so just for the luxury of jamming one bag so full of garbage that you need make only one trip to curb or alley.

Same goes for lunch, roasting bags, wet naps, and any other throw-aways. Be creative: Trade in your paper towels for old t-shirts. Try a little ammonia in water (or plain water for that matter) instead of commercial sprays to wash your windows.

Some things are not only reusable . . . some are worth money. Sell your empty aluminum cans to your local recycler; cans bring anywhere from 20¢ to 30¢ a pound. A summer's worth of cans for the average American family can easily be worth $20 or more.

Too little cash to be worth the bother? Becoming wealthy from scratch on an average (or less than average) income is a radical concept. It takes extreme measures to accomplish it. Every penny, nickel, or dime counts.

What will your neighbors say when they see your garage full of crushed aluminum cans? Or see you reusing foil? Or use rags instead of paper towels? Or line your garbage cans with paper bags from the grocery store instead of the maximum strength kind? Or, ugh, use cloth diapers?

Who cares what they say? But if they bug you, tell them you're doing your part for the ecology. That there is far too much waste. That we will run out of available garbage dumps by the year 2000 unless we take radical action. You'll become a hero for being willing to endure so much suffering for such a noble cause. And richer to boot.

I haven't mentioned that my wife came to this country about 15 years ago from a country outside the western hemisphere. When she arrived, a number of things about the American lifestyle didn't make sense to her.

One thing that she thought was particularly crazy was our waste of perfectly good containers. On the one hand, we would throw away perfectly good plastic food containers from the deli, grocery, or take-out restaurant while on the other hand we would spend money to buy similar containers for storage. Granted the store-bought kind were sturdier, but in her mind they were not worth the cost considering the abundance of free substitutes.

She cured me of my habit, and I confess our house is a rogues' gallery of free storage containers. We save virtually every kind from cups to mini-containers with lids for my lunchtime salad dressing. At first, when I opened my lunch bag I used to get a few looks, but no one pays attention any more. I guess they think I'm a bit odd. People call the same behavior in millionaires eccentricity. So join me—let's be eccentric!

Another thing my wife couldn't understand was why I bought ice from the store for our picnic cooler. She said, "Why buy something that we can have from home for free?" Discussions of convenience wouldn't budge her from her opinion.

She was and is right. Buying frozen water for $2 a bag is nuts. We found that by packing ice cubes from the freezer in smaller bundles of double plastic bags, sealed as air-tight as possible, our frozen water can outlast the store-bought kind. In fact, using good coolers we can keep ice for 24 hours or more. The Princess maintains that stores pack small cubes because they melt faster so you have to buy more. I say smaller cubes cool down drinks faster. I can relate more specifics on ice, but the point is that you can find a homemade solution to almost everything that costs money.

The object is to be able to save more of your income. The more money you save, the more money it will produce. So find the gold that's waiting for you in your closet, basement, garage, or garbage can. Turn time into money.

USE TIME TO YOUR ADVANTAGE

Speaking of time, have you ever noticed how salesmen for furnishings, appliances, autos, and other big ticket items are always trying to speed up your purchase decision? After a while they'll say something like this, "Mr. Jones, what will it take to get you to make your decision today?" In sales lingo this is called a trial close. Once you give an answer you have committed to the purchase according to the terms you stated.

Sounds okay, right? After all, you're telling him exactly what it will take for you to buy the item now. Buying now might be okay—if you have carefully researched the product and the range of prices charged for it. If, however, this is the first time you have dealt with this person or store, it is to your advantage to reverse the close and ask him to give *you* his best price. If he asks, "Then will you buy it?" You respond, "No, I need at least 24 hours to think about it. I never buy anything without thinking it over." If he refuses to give you a price, leave. If he gives you static or wants a deposit, repeat your terms and stand firm.

What you are doing is putting time to your psychological advantage. By delaying the purchase even for a day, you have put the thought in the salesman's mind that he might lose the sale; when you return, he will be more willing to negotiate. I caution you, however, that you must be sincere in your intent to purchase. You must assure him that you intend to buy and that you will come back to buy it from him. There's nothing a salesman hates more than a "tire kicker" who makes him jump through hoops and never buys anything.

On smaller items you can also use time to your advantage. Sooner or later everything goes on sale. The only thing you may lose by waiting is variety of choice. However, if the item is expensive even when it's on sale you usually still have a good selection.

The motto in the Trout household is: *"It's not for sale unless it's on sale."* Every member of our family knows it and lives by it. Copy it down and place it in strategic locations so you will make it your motto too!

Before my awakening, I believed getting a good deal was a trip to the land of blue-light specials. I learned, much to my surprise, that even better deals were waiting for me in the upscale department stores during their periodic sales and closeouts. The first skill I needed was the ability to recognize a deal when I saw it.

Deals Staring Us in the Eye

I told you that when I was out of work the Princess and I did a lot of recreational shopping. That is, we did a great deal of looking with little or no buying. It was the only recreation we could afford, but we also received a marvelous education for our efforts. When I returned to work, this knowledge allowed us to make some great buys.

Shopping tours are a good idea for you, too. Do lots of looking. Look at the prices of things you're not presently in the market for. You never know when a bargain will present itself. If you have no knowledge of an item's value, real bargains will be invisible. Learn all the brand names and price ranges of top-quality clothes, shoes, and furnishings. During clearance sales, these items will often be reduced by up to 80% of the retail price.

Find manufacturer outlets and check their prices against the prices of the same items on sale in department or wholesale outlets. Shop for everything you purchase, from insurance policies to airfares. Never buy anything for the first price you find. In addition, look for substitute products. Is there a look-alike product that is of similar quality, but at half the price? Don't fall in love with one brand; have a second brand that you are willing to buy if the price is right!

DEVELOPING X-RAY VISION

Marketers spend millions of dollars building brand awareness in buyers' minds. They research population statistics called demographics to determine who's most likely to purchase their products. They know their buyers' age, sex, marital and family status, highest level of education attained, and household income. They know what part of the country they live in and whether it's city, small town, or rural. They further subdivide or segment their buying population by frequency and size of purchase and by psychological factors and social influences they believe will trigger purchases.

That's why a certain cigarette uses cowboys in its ads while another uses young, independent-looking, professionally-dressed women. An entire campaign may be devoted to a current social attitude like "The Me Generation." Marketers know that they need more than great taste or value to sell their products; they also need a strong emotional appeal that roots itself in our need to belong, be accepted, save work or time, or enhance our opportunities for love, sex, money, or recognition. They don't push saving money, except for a few products in the budget category unless merchants are overstocked and business is bad!

Don't believe it? Have you ever seen ugly models touting the value and price of a cosmetic? Or dorky male models telling you what a great deal they got on the latest in men's fashions? Of course not! Marketers play on our fantasies, subtly implying, "Maybe if I wear this he or she will notice me," or, "In that car my friends and neighbors will know how successful I am."

You'll never be rich if you allow your financial decisions to be run by your emotions. You must develop x-ray vision to see through the hype to the basic product value. Rid yourself once and for all of brand consciousness—even if you can prove there's reason for you to prefer a particular brand.

Once you are able to drink any kind of pop, beer, wine, juice, or whatever as long as it's on sale, you've beaten the system. Lack of preference is a great equalizer. It makes all products indistinguishable except for price.

Once you reach this acceptance level you'll make a shocking discovery. House brands, regional or local brands, generics, and seconds are often of the same or higher quality than the name brand.

A friend of mine who used to work in a cannery told me that all canned vegetables were the same. The only thing that changed were the labels. I don't know if this is really true, but I can tell you that my taste buds can't tell the difference.

Much of marketing is based on herd psychology: Once something is accepted or fashionable everyone wants to do it. Take the athletic-shoe craze. Where I live, working women often wear a pair of athletic shoes and socks over their nylons. When they get to work they change to their dress shoes. It's fashionable to wear a certain brand of athletic shoes and a certain type of socks.

I reasoned that this trend must have started out of a need for comfort. I was wrong. It started in New York when the Brooklyn Bridge was closed for repairs. Although auto, bus, and truck traffic was stopped, pedestrian traffic was unhampered. Commuting workers who used buses, cabs, and cars faced long and time-consuming detours. Some plucky gals donned their athletic shoes and walked the expanse of bridge to save time. Before the bridge was reopened thousands of athletic-shod women were walking. The trend swept the nation.

There's absolutely nothing wrong with wearing athletic shoes. In fact, they're probably good for your feet. The point is: Don't get unconsciously caught up in any movements, trends, or fashions. Do it because you have thought it over and have decided that it is good for you. Then use your x-ray vision to find the best deal possible.

Boil every purchase down to its simplest unit. See the wood beneath the veneer.

Separating Fool's Gold from 24 Karat

During your shopping tours, make sure that you're making apple-to-apple comparisons. If similar products are packaged in different-sized boxes, both of which are labeled large, make a realistic cost determination by reducing costs to a unit of common measure like pennies per pound or dollars per yard. Many stores have already done this for you with shelf-markers that show both total cost and comparative cost based on the largest unit of common measure: Ounces, quarts, etc. If your stores don't do this you can still determine the actual cost of two different sized packages by dividing the price of each by its quantity (see Figure 4-1). Sometimes you'll find that a larger size isn't a better deal.

Figure 4-1: Apple to Apple Comparison

Bigger isn't always a better deal. Look. . .

Which is a better deal: Box A or Box B?

Cereal A

Size = Giant
Weight = 1 lb. 4 oz. = 20 oz.
Price = $1.70

Cereal B

Size = Extra Large
Weight = 1 lb. 13 oz. = 29 oz.
Price - $2.79

Cost per ounce:

$1.70 ÷ 20 oz. = 8.5¢/oz. $2.79 ÷ 29 oz. = 9.62¢/oz.

9.62 - 8.50 = 1.12 cents per ounce savings.

You'll save 22¢ by buying the 20 ounce box instead of the larger box.

What if one store charges by count and another store charges for the same item by weight like bananas by the pound or by the bunch? You must compare units on a common basis. It is always better to compare with a standard unit of measure like weight instead of a measure of quantity like a dozen, because the size of individual items may vary. Ask the store selling bananas by the bunch to weigh them. Then divide the cost by the weight. You will easily be able to compare the prices (see Figure 4-2). If it will help you, carry a pocket calculator to do the calculations. (Buy the solar-powered kind to save on batteries.)

Extreme? You bet, but it's the only accurate way to determine the true value of a product. To be successful in your struggle for wealth you need to apply these techniques to all your purchases. Think purchases through to their logical conclusions no matter how good they look. For instance, are extended warranties worth the cost? With the cost of a major repair running upwards to hundreds if not thousands of dollars, at first glance you might say definitely yes. I'm not convinced.

Figure 4-2: Like-Unit Comparisons

Which is a better deal: Bananas at Store A or Store B?

Store A

Bananas = 29¢ per lb.

Store B

Bananas = $1.00 per bunch

Step One:

Determine the cost per pound for the store selling bananas by the bunch by dividing their cost by their total weight in ounces. For example, the bunch in Store B weighed 2 lbs. 10 oz. or 42 oz.

$1.00 ÷ 42 oz. = .0238 per oz.

Step Two:

Multiply the ounce rate by 16 to determine the cost per pound. Example:

.0238¢ x 16 oz. = .38¢ per lb.

Answer:

In this case the bananas sold by the pound were cheaper, but this is not always the case. To be sure you're getting the best deal, always compare prices based on like units of measure.

For one thing automotive manufacturers have had to extend their warranties to remain competitive and most now offer at least a three-year, 36,000-mile motor-train warranty. Some offer considerably longer warranty terms.

No, motor-train warranties don't include all those little annoying do-dads that always seem to break after the comprehensive portion of the warranty has ended, but they do cover probably the greatest sources of the most expensive repairs. However, you must carefully read your car's warranty to determine precisely what is or is not covered. From my perspective with so many things routinely covered under new car warranties now it's hard to justify an extended warranty's additional cost. In fact, with extended warranty prices starting at $500 you've got a big bite to make up before they start paying for themselves.

WAREHOUSING: HOW TO AMPLIFY BARGAINS

You run into a great sale; the highest quality shoes are 75% off list. You know you can't even buy cheap shoes for the same price. What do you do?

You buy but not just one or two pairs but enough shoes to last you for several years. Inflation has been around a long time and will continue to remain an economic reality as long as our government continues to mint currency without any standard of value other than a promise of good faith. So rest assured that even if you match the discount you get today, the price tomorrow will be higher!

So buy five, six, however many pairs of shoes you'd normally use during the next three years and pay cash for them. What you are doing is what many good businesses do: They warehouse supplies to optimize favorable discounts. You can apply the same concept to purchases of food, clothing, and supplies for your home.

For clothing the key to warehousing success is purchasing items that are standards or classics, things that won't go out of style quickly. Usually items that fall in this category are high-quality garments that are conservatively styled, like men's wing-tip shoes and pin-striped suits that are always in good taste.

For growing children, you can take advantage of special sales and save dollars for today and tomorrow. Extend your discount by buying the same outfit, jacket, pants, or dress, in different colors and sizes. By doing this you will avoid the worst kind of purchasing there is—buying things when you need them!

Cleaning agents, toothpaste, soap, detergents are storable for years as long as you don't buy them in aerosol cans which may lose their propellants. Canned food, fruit, and pop last a year or more. Toilet paper, tissues, and light bulbs are good indefinitely. Even bread, rolls, cakes, and other bakery items can be frozen for a month or more. Stock up when the price is right.

Must Be a Party

Recently one of our local grocery chains had a pre-Labor Day Special on cola by the case. The limit was three cases per customer. So my wife and I, each with our own cart, headed to the pop aisle. She had collected some dollar-off coupons which dropped the case price to $3.88, or 16¢ per can. She had collected ten coupons, so we would need to return to the store one additional time to use all our coupons.

As I was loading the sixth case into her cart, a fellow shopper commented, "You two going to have a big party this weekend?" I replied, "Yeah, we have a party every weekend!" Although it was nearly half its regular price, this woman just couldn't think of any reason other than a big party why I would buy so much pop. I would have liked to tell her that I was stocking up for several months, but I knew that she wouldn't understand.

Next time you see someone buying lots of anything, go check out the price. It could be a good deal, but you don't have to wait for sales if you buy in volume. This is particularly true of fresh fruits and vegetables. Grocery stores will give you a case price on many items if you ask for it. If they are over-stocked, sometimes you get a terrific buy. Of course, to optimize the discount you need to warehouse the buy. How do you do this with perishables? Can and freeze them yourself.

My friend's mother is from Greece. She uses a great deal of lemon juice in cooking and has found a novel way to warehouse fresh lemon juice. She buys lemons by the case in the winter when they are cheap and squeezes the juice into ice trays and freezes them. The cubes she transfers to freezer bags. Anytime she wants fresh lemon juice, she thaws out a cube.

Find ways to warehouse everything you need from clothing to automobile antifreeze. Learn how to inventory perishables. Every time you'll be paying yourself for the effort.

EVERYTHING IS NEGOTIABLE

One of the most profitable money-saving techniques is one I found very hard to do. That was asking for a deal. I used to ask meekly for a price concession, but I would never insist on a deal before I bought an item or service. True, I was a fairly good negotiator when it came to buying a car because I knew the bargaining was expected behavior in car showrooms. But I would never ask for a deal anywhere else. I had convinced myself that it was inappropriate and cheap to do so. Truth was, I was more worried about what complete strangers would think of me than about my own financial welfare.

My wife cured me of this by some astonishing examples of just how negotiable the prices of things really are. I used to tell her with embarrassment, "We don't do that in this country!" when she would ask for a better price. I was wrong! The following experience cured me forever of being afraid to ask for a deal!

Shortly after we were married, I needed some dress shirts so my wife and I visited the shirt shop I had dealt with for many years. The shirts were on sale for 25% off the list price. I felt 25% was a bargain considering their quality and fit, and the fact that their list price was already several dollars cheaper than comparable brands. Humbly, however, I asked if there was any better deal. The store owner said absolutely not.

My wife stepped forward. She said, "Are you telling me that if we buy four shirts you won't give us a better deal?" He said no. She persisted: "How about five shirts? Six shirts?" When she reached eight shirts, he weakened saying, "What kind of deal do you want?" The negotiations commenced with discounts ranging from 30% to 75% being argued back and forth. We settled on a deal of 50% off, if we bought all eight and paid cash instead of using a credit card. (Merchants have to pay the credit card company a percentage of the sale every time you use a card. The percentage ranges from 2.5% to 7% depending on the card used.)

The moral to the story is that everything is negotiable. To get the best price, keep asking for it and after each turndown keep raising the size of your order until you get a response. Then you negotiate your terms using all your powers of observation to guarantee that what you are being offered is the best deal. If a merchant is adamant in selling things on his terms look elsewhere for bargains. If he has the absolutely best price, go back and buy it. Just don't be afraid to ask even if you get a snotty response.

Usually the more expensive the item, the greater the willingness to negotiate the price. For example, car, truck, boat, and R.V. dealers are almost always willing to negotiate price, because the pay interest (or in their terms "juice") on their inventories. These inventory programs are called dealer floor plans. The interest charged to dealers under these programs by manufacturers and banks is expensive, anywhere from two to four points above the prime interest rate. At the writing of this book the prime rate interest was 9%.

You can use knowledge of this to your advantage. Ask the dealer for the oldest inventoried cars. Tell him that as long as the car has the basic equipment you want, you're not fussy about the color. He'll gladly show you these cars, because they are costing him a fortune to keep.

Another thing I've found helpful is to time your new purchases toward the end of the month. Salesmen have quotas and tiered commission structures. Many times they're one or two items short of reaching the next commission or bonus level. Your sale may mean the difference between a big and a small bonus, making him more willing to fight with his management for a better deal for you.

The same goes for dealers. Dealers often get financial incentives from the manufacturers for selling so many cars during a period. The last few days of a quarter are one of the better times to buy. Another good time to buy is when dealers are offering special rebates and bonuses. During these special promotions they will be less willing to give you a deal beyond the rebate, but don't let them buffalo you. The reason they are offering the rebate in the first place is because their business stinks. This is absolutely the best time to get a great deal, but you'll have to push for it!

I've been with my wife to the same dealer ten to fifteen times before buying anything. We've negotiated a single car or boat deal for hours. The key to winning is your willingness not to buy if your terms aren't met. Eventually if you don't get just what you want, you'll still get a much better deal.

Cars, boats, and shirts aren't all that are negotiable.[1] Legal, stock, and real estate fees are also negotiable. The key to getting a better deal on the first two is letting the lawyer or broker know that you plan on using him exclusively for all your business and that you have plenty of work. If you need a lawyer for a house closing, also ask the price of additional service like a will. Then ask what kind of deal he'll give you if you let him do both.

My full-service stock broker charges me $50 a trade. He makes his money on the difference between the bid and ask price. His price is cheaper than the discount broker I used to use. How did I get such a deal? I asked for it!

Any time you buy a costly item or service ask for a deal. Try to negotiate a price by buying additional products or services, promising more business, or accepting the price and negotiating additional features at no additional cost.

---

[1] *Homes and real estate negotiations will be discussed in Chapter Eight.*

The Pen Is Mightier

Sometimes you must negotiate from weakness. By this I mean that the person you are doing business with has reneged on your deal and you are about to lose money. Almost as good as saving money is not losing any.

When an agreement collapses, your first inclination may be to sue somebody. If that somebody happens to be a big corporation, think again. Corporations have armies of lawyers and fat legal budgets. The best way to deal with these folks is first to know your legal rights and whether or not their actions break any laws that could result in court orders that will restrain or end their business activities. A second way is to understand the power of the written word and how you can use public relations to your advantage.

I have had many great knowledge-building part-time jobs. One was selling life insurance for a major carrier. Insurance sales are licensed by the state, so I had to pass a long, complex test on insurance law to get my license. My studies for this test taught me a lot.

Several years later I was working for a magazine publisher. My secretary was a young woman with three children. She had struggled financially all her life. Then disaster struck. Her husband had a prolonged illness and died. They had taken personal loans out to cover expenses even before he became ill. With one of the larger loans they had also purchased the optional life insurance.

After the funeral she called the loan company to find out how to apply for the life insurance coverage to clear the loan. She explained that her husband had died of kidney disease. They asked how long he had had it and she told them. The manager replied that since his condition preceded the policy start date, it was a "pre-existing condition" and therefore was not covered by the policy.

She told me what had happened. I remembered my insurance law, which stated that if a person lives for two years after a life insurance policy has been in effect it will be payable regardless of any "pre-existing conditions." I called the manager to tell him of this. He would not listen. I called the State Superintendent of Insurance for the exact wording of the law. It was given to me—along with a message for the loan company which said in essence that if they did not comply with the code their license to operate would be forfeited.

When I apprised the manager, he said they would get back to us. They did. They paid up my secretary's loan.

Hit 'Em Where They Hurt

Sometimes you have to use a little imagination to settle money-losing situations. These are usually times when the situation involves bureaucracy or obstinate business partners.

Once I got caught in a single insurance company's red tape and it almost cost me $3,000, at a time when such a loss would have been devastating. I was changing jobs and was also about to incur some hospital expenses. Knowing my new company's medical plan had a probationary period before I would be covered, I made arrangements with my former employer to stay with his policy for the interim. The same insurance carrier covered both companies but from different state groups: My former employer's group was in New York. My new employer's group was in Illinois.

When I went to submit my bills to my former employer's group they refused to accept them, saying that the policy had been canceled. I told them that I had paid for the coverage and never had canceled the policy. They told me that when I signed up with my new company's group they automatically canceled my former policy. I submitted the bills to the new company.

They refused to pay them because the bills were incurred prior to my coverage start date.

Since I couldn't get anyone to listen, I wrote-up a press release entitled "A Tale of Two Policies—A Modern Insurance Horror Story" detailing how insensitive bureaucratic bungling was cheating poor little Mr. John Q. Public out of his entitled coverage. Included was the list of the TV stations and newspapers to which I planned to mail the release. High on my list were stations and papers in both their geographic areas. I read the release to company reps over the telephone. I didn't have to go any further. They agreed to settle the claim internally.

For big companies the threat of bad public relations is potent. Lawyers don't scare them as much as lost sales, depressed stock prices, and the chance of some costly government investigation resulting from scandalous coverage in the news media.

I used the same strategy when the owner of a house I bought failed to pay for the repair of damage he had concealed. He took a "so go ahead and sue me" attitude. My lawyer advised me that suing would mean a long, drawn-out battle where even if I won I would lose in terms of legal fees. We held up the closing until my lawyer came up with a bright idea. Since the real estate broker wouldn't earn a dime unless we closed, we decided to negotiate with them for payment of the repairs out of their commission. We did and closed the deal.

However, later I found out that the repairs were going to be more extensive. I approached the broker. He said the deal was closed and they had lived up to their part of the bargain. He wouldn't budge.

So I mailed him a series of letters capitalizing on the theme that he was in a neighborhood business and that an unhappy customer can be very harmful to his business because his business is promoted by word of mouth more than any other way. Each letter became increasingly more activist. The last letter explained that I wouldn't be able to contain myself when neighbors asked me what I thought of their agency. The last letter did it. They asked for an estimate and paid the bill.

I've used creative strategies with a utility company, an auto manufacturer, and a car wash to settle on potential losses. Don't allow yourself to be cheated. Determine your legal rights, define the seat of power, and plan your approach. Be persistent but polite. Most important: Use your gray matter!

BECOME A GROCER'S NIGHTMARE

No more one-stop shopping! Become a grocer's nightmare, shopping only for promotional or loss-leader items. Many times grocers will offer items below cost to get you into the store. Grocers know that most shoppers will do their entire week's worth of shopping once they are there.

Change the way you usually shop. Instead of planning your week's menu and then shopping, read the grocery sales sheets and then plan your menu. Eat what's on sale. If the same things are on sale as last week, be creative in your preparation. Make sure you use coupons and rebates wherever possible!

One final note: The new computerized registers make mistakes. This is particularly true the day before a sale is over. The easiest way to catch these mistakes is not to buy more than ten items at a time. Watch the prices as they are registered. Speak up if the wrong price is entered, and check your receipt before you leave for home.

Rebates—Wringing Out the Last Nickel

Rebates combined with sale prices are magic. Be sure to check at the service desk before you leave the store for any rebates. Sometimes rebates can really pay you for buying the product.

Once we needed antifreeze for our car. A new brand was being introduced. My wife found $3.50 rebates for two gallons of this antifreeze. A builders supply store offered the brand on a special sale of two gallons for $10, nearly $8 off the regular price. Coupled with the rebate our total savings were $11.50, or $5.75 per gallon. Looking at it from another angle, we were able to buy eight gallons of antifreeze for the price of three gallons at the regular price.

One of our best rebate deals ever was on decorative garden stones. At a hardware store at the end of the season we found seven bags of decorative stones that had been broken open. None of the bags was completely full, but what was left probably equaled a good five and a half bags. The bags were marked down to $2 each. My wife convinced them to take a buck each if we took the lot. They agreed.

On the side of each bag was a $1.50 per bag rebate coupon that hadn't expired so we carefully complied with all the rebate requirements—including forwarding the store receipt. Considering the price we had paid, we knew we might get an argument so we kept the company's address and local telephone number. Several weeks passed and no rebate. I telephoned. They knew who I was and were shocked that I would ask for the rebate considering what I had paid for the stones. I reminded them that their offer had no mention of a required purchase price and that they were bound by law to comply.

They didn't like it, but a few days later we received a check for $10.50. We had actually made a $3.50 profit for purchasing the stones. Mind you, this may be a unique experience, but it shows how a combination of negotiating skills, sale prices, rebates, and persistence can move you along the road to riches.

However, there are a few crooks out there who won't play by the rules—or rather, they will make the rules impossible to comply with. We had an experience with a vodka distiller. The distiller offered a $1.50 rebate. We bought the vodka on sale, so the rebate was a nice added bonus. The instructions were to soak the label off the neck and return it with the store receipt. The bottle was made of plastic and the label glue wouldn't come off. We decided to saw off the bottle neck with the label and mail it as one unit. Although the postage would be half the rebate, it was still worth it. We never received the rebate. It is obvious to us that the distiller had planned it that way.

There's only one way to beat crooks like this. Vote with your feet! Never buy another product of theirs and tell everyone about your experience. *Oh, vodka distiller, are you listening?*

CHAPTER **5**

From Poor Immigrant to Rich Citizen in Ten Years or Less

They come from Viet Nam, Korea, Pakistan, India, Greece, Africa, Europe, Canada, South America, and Mexico. But no matter where they come from, they seem able to accomplish something that seems to defy native-born Americans . . . they're able to become wealthy quickly, regardless of the economic conditions at the time of their arrival.

How can they do it when we who have lived here all our lives can't? That question has always bothered me. It does so even more today with the many tensions and influences that threaten our financial security.

Every day immigrants come to this country who seem to have a special ability to achieve financial success. Many who lack education, language skills, and money are still able to achieve success.

How do they do it? I decided that the only way to find out was to ask them.

THEY LAUGHED WHEN I ASKED HOW THEY DID IT

I've asked many wealthy new Americans how they achieved their great success, and with few exceptions my question drew a laugh. The modest or shrewd ones tell me either it was hard work or they don't know—luck maybe. The bolder ones retort, "You mean to tell me *you* don't know?"

If I press them for an answer their responses usually follow a common theme, "We do things that native-born Americans won't do!" Things like living with two or three families in the same house with all adult members working and sharing household duties. Things like holding two or three jobs at the same time, all with the primary goal of saving as much as possible out of what is earned.

Immigrant groups see work only as an opportunity to improve their lives. They'll take on any and all openings available to them, be it in factories, hospitals, or restaurants, or driving a cab. Moreover, they'll work as many hours as they are physically able. They gladly accept positions that Americans would feel are beneath them and are constantly on the lookout for ways to improve themselves.

Thrift is a way of life for them, even those who come to America with advanced degrees and find high-paying jobs. Most important, they have different values about what is important in life and definitely are more money-motivated.

Why are they like this? It would be easy to say that they are like this because they come from poor countries and for them America is a paradise. But this would not be entirely true. Although thrift and dedication to work have always been an American immigrant heritage, I think that a better answer lies in how they measure their success. To most of them success is measured in terms of money power. They are less thing-oriented than Americans; unlike Americans they measure wealth in terms of savings. Saving has value to them in and of itself. And unlike their former homelands, America offers them greater wealth-building opportunities.

Americans who are born here have a narrower view. We measure wealth in terms of our ability to buy things. If our purchasing power goes down we feel poorer. Our measure is rooted in purchasing not savings power. Furthermore we tend to have a parochial rather than a global perspective. We assess our financial success in terms of how much better off we are than our relatives, friends and associates, neighbors, or own personal past history. We rarely, if ever, compare ourselves to others outside the U.S. like the average European, Asian, or African. This tendency blinds us to the reality that America is still a wealthy nation by world standards and that our measure of poverty is definitely not poverty elsewhere in the world.

Furthermore Americans' point of reference is too image-related. We are more worried about looking good than about being in good financial shape. Our image consciousness camouflages opportunities that are right before our eyes, opportunities that are abundantly clear to newcomers here.

After talking to many immigrants, I decided that they could teach me a great deal about how to save.

Getting Maximum Value

"Would you pay $500 for a 19" black and white television set?" No, this is not a trick question. It is a comparative example of just how expensive some things are. Things that we routinely buy without much thought. It's based on our inclination to accept outrageously extravagant prices in small purchases that at the same inflated level we would not accept in larger purchases.

Take gum. At the candy counter a single pack of five sticks retails for 40¢. Not a major purchase consideration— unless you consider the fact that you can buy a bag of ten packs on sale for 89¢. So what you are paying at the candy counter is a 500% premium for a single pack. Another way to think about it is that over ten days worth of gum purchases you've paid $3.11 for absolutely nothing.

New immigrants are keenly aware of this type of price disparity and take great measures to avoid it. For example, whoever said that you have to buy your pop at the fast food restaurant when you buy a burger there? Granted it takes some guts to bring your own pop into your local fast food eatery, but you'll save 200% to 300% over the price of buying it there. Same goes for the movies, sports events, and rock concerts. Bring your own popcorn and candy. (If you're easily embarrassed, carry them in a large purse.) The inflated prices you pay for these items in theaters, stadiums, and arenas is outrageous!

As badly inflated as these prices are, they pale in comparison to the prices you pay for alcoholic beverages at your favorite restaurant or lounge. This is particularly true for mixed drinks and wine by the bottle, where the cost differential over beverages enjoyed at home can exceed 600%.

I know, I know . . . you just love those olives and pickled mushrooms they serve with your martinis. You better love 'em. Separated from the booze, they cost you 35¢ to 50¢ each. You can buy an entire jar of olives and pickled mushrooms for about the same price as one martini alone.

The only way to deflate these extraordinary costs is by purchasing your liquor on sale and drinking it at home. Have a drink-in. You'll enjoy premium quality for far less than the cheap stuff bought out.

Eating out also costs more than eating at home. Make it a policy to eat out rarely but when you do, eat out on special promotions only. Like "buy one, get one free" deals. If you have a kid under five years of age, don't buy those cute little kid dinners, especially the ones at the fast food places. They are tremendously overpriced. Use discretion in what you order for your children; kids waste half of what's on their plates anyway. For children three and under ask for an extra plate and share your meal with your kid.

Got a kid with a huge appetite? Get an adult meal that's on special and doggy bag half of it before he eats. You'll have a second meal ready for tomorrow and be dollars ahead to boot!

You can make similar savings while travelling by bringing easy-to-prepare meals along with you. Breakfast cereals, coffee cakes, donuts can be easily carried and will save you a bundle over hotel and restaurant breakfasts. Milk for cereal can be carried in small pop bottles with screw caps.

You can save money on lunches as well. Bring along a supply of rolls, pickles, chips, and condiments. Shop for lunch meats, cheeses, and side dish salads from local supermarket delis along the way. Prudent shopping can yield travelling picnic lunches for four to five people for under $5. All will stay fresh thanks to picnic coolers filled with free ice courtesy of your hotel ice machine. Even hot cups of coffee or tea can be inexpensively prepared in the privacy of your room with a low-cost, 2- to 4-cup hot pot.

True, I've seen this carried to extremes by thrifty foreign travellers. One morning on a business trip I was awakened by voices outside my room. I peered out my window and was shocked to see 20 to 30 foreign travelers cooking on barbecue grills on the lawn in front of the motel.

I called the front desk to find out what was going on. I was told that a bus from Mexico had pulled in with a tour group who were scheduled to spend the next few days at the hotel. Although the driver spoke little English, he was the designated spokesman for the group. Being early in the morning, the clerk routinely asked how many they should set up for breakfast. Only the words "breakfast" and "set up" made it through the translation. Immediately the entire group headed for the bus, whereupon all broke out their picnic coolers and grills and proceeded to make breakfast. We business travelers were appalled, but the tourists were unmoved and contently carried on making and enjoying their breakfast right there on the front lawn of a busy Holiday Inn.

I give the example because most of us would be mortified to cook breakfast on the lawn of a hotel. But in a wealth-building program no idea should be immediately discarded, because typically it's the unorthodox things that have the greatest wealth potential. If we fear trying these things because of the possibility of being criticized, we diminish our opportunity.

Give up those fears! As long as the fear of embarrassment or criticism guides you, you can never be wealthy on your current income. These thoughts limit your wealth-building options. You must instead strive to expand them.

An area to start with is those items that go on sale after you bought them. I can hear the groans! How many times have you bought an item only to have it go on sale the next day or week? A more important question is: What did you do about it?

What can you do? Take it back! Yes, *take it back!* Why should you suffer a loss because a purchase was poorly timed? Return the item for cash and buy it again. If you're gutsy, do the complete transaction at the same register. Be bold!

The same goes for items that don't live up to their expected performance. If a product falls apart during normal use in less than its expected life, take it back, even if you've had it several months. Better stores guarantee your satisfaction. Make sure you get it. This is particularly true for items with long or lifetime guarantees.

Product warranties often aren't exercised, because product owners mislay sales receipts and warranty certificates. To avoid this happening to you, make a file exclusively for warranties. When you buy anything, religiously deposit the warranty and sales receipt in this file. This alone can save you hundreds if not thousands of dollars. We've had mattresses, chairs, and appliances that failed to perform after several years of service repaired or replaced free. We've even had items that were out of warranty replaced in part or full.

A case in point involves an expensive watch of mine. I bought the watch on sale along with a bonus certificate for lifetime battery replacements. Over the life of the watch, the batteries are worth several hundred dollars, so taken together with the sale price, I felt I had got a significant bargain. I've had the watch for several years and have had batteries replaced twice. A couple of weeks after the most recent battery replacement, I noticed that the crystal was cracked. I am very careful with my things and most certainly would have noticed it if I had bumped into something that would have cracked the crystal. The only thing I could figure was that the crystal must have been cracked when the jeweler replaced the battery. Since it had been several weeks since I had picked up the watch I really couldn't insist it was their fault, but it was certainly worth mentioning.

I showed the jeweler the watch and offered my theory on what had happened. He agreed it was odd the way the crystal was cracked and also agreed that it could have happened as I suggested. I was careful not to blame them. Rather I suggested the possibility of shared responsibility. At the time of our discussion I also happened to be looking at several new watches.

The manager told me a new crystal would be $100, but they would split the cost with me fifty/fifty. I knew I would be without a watch for several weeks so I made them an offer: "Fix my watch for free and I'll buy another watch." They agreed and we both made out.

It's Better if It's Free

My Jewish friends taught me a wonderful Yiddish word: *shnorring. Shnorring* means getting something for free. There's no better way to build wealth.

There are lots of a ways to shnorr but a good time is during purchase negotiations. If you're buying a car, negotiate your lowest price—then ask them to throw in a set of mats, touch-up paint, free oil changes, a full tank of gas, anything that might be considered an incidental to the dealer but is worth real dollars to you. By incidental I mean items that may cost anywhere from $10 to $100. Try not to get too greedy. Asking them to throw in big things will blow the deal. Keep them small but get as many of them as you can. These little extras will appreciably enhance the value of your deal.

You can use the same strategy for jewelry, furniture, or appliances. Again settle on a price, then ask them to throw in some extras like jewelry cleaner, polish, padding, or set-up. Ask for free delivery, covers, cases, whatever. You might even try something that involves no direct cost to them, but would be extremely valuable to you. For instance, when we bought our boat, since we had no boating experience, we knew we would need some "on the water" training. As part of our purchase agreement we negotiated six hours worth of free instructions from the general manager. He was a good fellow and there was no direct cost to him, so he gladly agreed to this.

Free samples are also wonderful to shnorr. In this case, the manufacturer wants you to try his product and will not balk if you ask for more than one sample. In fact, I've found that you can get a lot more if you keep asking until he says no. Then ask, "How about a couple more for my mother, aunt, cousin, etc.,?" Keep the banter light and funny. Usually you'll get what you want.

Doctors have sample medicines. Dentists have toothbrushes and toothpaste samples. Perfume counters have lotion, powder, and perfume samples. Ask for them. If you're a great shnorrer you may never have to buy them. However, no matter what your level of ability is, by getting anything free you are dollars ahead!

Gambling—Sucker's Style? Or Winner's?

I'm not a real gambler in any sense of the word. However, where there's no cost, I'll take a chance. After all, I've got nothing to lose. Fill out every contest entry blank you find. You never know; you might win.

I must report that my winnings record to date is not very good: One giant stuffed Santa Claus, a cheap camera, and a $50 gift certificate from a local children's clothier. But these wins put me ahead of the game and the gift certificate came during the time I was out of work. It's a gift that I am very thankful for to this day.

One Caveat: The current contest craze has brought some unscrupulous marketers into the arena. Their latest gimmick is to mail authentic-looking redemption certificates claiming that you have definitely won one of the prizes listed on the certificate. The prize list is crowded with expensive prizes with a few token cheap gifts seeded in. The certificate reassures you that you definitely have won and that all you need to do to claim your prize is to call for an appointment to pick it up at the redemption center. If you bite, you have reserved an appointment for a lengthy high-pressure sales pitch for some service or product like a time-share vacation condo.

If you don't remember filling out a registration blank for the contest, then you probably didn't. Forget about the certificates. You can expect to receive three to four reminders after the first one. Each one will implore you to take immediate action or else you'll forfeit your valuable prize. Forget it.

What about lotteries? If you must gamble at lotteries, buy only one ticket. Your odds of winning do not change whether you buy one or a thousand tickets. Feel lucky today? You'd be safer if you stay at home instead of going out to buy a lottery ticket! With five chances out of a million of being struck by lightning, you have a better chance of being hit by a random bolt than becoming a lottery millionaire. If you don't believe me just look at the odds listed on the back of the ticket. Don't be a sucker. Buy one ticket a week or a month. Don't be suckered into buying any more. If you win, I wish you great happiness. If you don't win, you're still a winner because you haven't wasted any more than a couple of dollars.

HOW NOT TO BE PENNY WISE AND POUND FOOLISH

I'm sure you all know someone who wastes more money getting bargains than they're worth. This can happen to us too if we're not careful. The easiest way to avoid this is by calculating all the costs of securing a deal. That includes the gas to get there and back.

Avoid the temptation of assuming you'll find good bargains just because you're planning to buy from a manufacturer's outlet, outlet mall, or wholesale club. With respect to wholesale clubs and other stores that charge a membership fee, I expect to recoup my entire membership fee in discounts greater than I could get from other stores. And I expect to recoup my investment within a trip or two, otherwise the membership isn't worth the cost. The reason for my feeling is that you have no guarantee that prices will remain at the same low rate as when you purchased the membership. Over time prices will be adjusted upwards. If they rise beyond the discounted prices in regular stores, your membership will actually cost you more than what it is worth.

Outlet malls are the latest rage in my area. These new malls offer everything regular stores do but at discounted prices. An exploratory trip is worth the gas, but make the trip worthwhile by taking along a pad of paper and a pencil. Buy only the items you know are great deals. For others that you're unsure of, write down the manufacturer, the style or model number, and the price. When you return compare the prices you've written down with similar sale items in local stores.

I've done this myself and have found that I can often get as good a price for the same items on sale in regular department stores or wholesale stores near my home. Since many of the manufacturer's outlets are a distance from my home I enjoy additional savings on gas by buying locally. An added benefit of buying in regular stores is that the items are easier to return if I experience any problems or they're further reduced in price.

Many of the items offered in outlets are final-sale-only items, which means you can't return them.

TAKING THE HEAT OUT OF UTILITY BILLS

My evening stroll takes me past neighboring homes ablaze with light. Every room is pleasantly aglow with warm light from lamps, ceiling fixtures, and indirect lighting. A lovely scene, replete with subtle garden and coach lights. I love to look at them yet wonder what kind of electric bills these folks must pay.

I'm all for lighting for security purposes, but from a wealth-building, or even from an ecological, standpoint, there's no reason to light the whole house. Every dark room represents dollars in your pocket. Turn the lights off and get every member to cooperate. While you're at it install lower wattage bulbs. Most folks can use half the wattage they are presently using.

Beyond electric lights, think about how you use the other things that affect your utility bills. Take the oven. Whenever my wife uses it, she finds a way to cook several things at once. When a roast is almost done, for instance, she puts the vegetables she would normally boil on top of the stove in an oven-safe container and "boil" them inside the oven. The first time I saw her do it I thought it was madness, but our average monthly electric bills of $38 to $48 proves to me she's on to something. That's $38 to $48 a month in the Midwest for an eight-room two-story home with an electric stove and an electronic security system.

We are just as frugal in our use of heat, air conditioning, and water as we are with electricity. Nothing is automatic in our house. We consider utilities as products for sale like anything else. When we turn on a light or use an appliance, we are buying the energy to run it. This includes indirect uses of utilities like the heat energy used by the water heater. Beside turning it down to 145°F, we also take short, low-pressure showers. Same for the gas furnace. Lowering the thermostat puts dollars in your pocket!

Utilities never go on sale, but you can contain costs by regulating when and how you use them. Often the time utilities are used affects the cost as much as how much energy is used. For peak usage times power companies charge premiums and other times utilities, like phone companies, offer discounts. The key to savings is reducing usage during premium rate times and transferring usage to periods when discounts are offered.

For heating and air conditioning, smart users not only dial down, they also close off rooms they're not using. They confine energy use to actual living areas and supplement reduced energy use with blankets, sweaters, or slippers in the winter, and shorts, swim suits, and fans in the summer. You don't have to be uncomfortable to reduce utility costs, you just have to be smarter in how you use them.

Some friends of mine think they're saving money by cutting down the heat at night and using electric blankets instead. While I grant that they probably are saving some money by localizing their energy use to the blanket, a better way to save more money is to replace the electric blanket with a down comforter. What about your head? Wear a stocking cap!

Crazy? No . . . extreme is a much better word! I don't need the cap, but I have awakened with a cold nose. Aren't you more prone to sickness with reduced heat and air conditioning? Since we started cutting back on the heat and air conditioning we've had fewer colds and less flu.

Conserve as much heat as possible. Drafty doors and windows can be easily sealed with caulking. Attics can be insulated with blow-in glass insulation that will pay for itself after the first heating season. It's easy to determine whether or not your house needs to have the attic insulated: On a snowy day take a look at your roof. If it's covered with a nice layer of snow, your attic is properly insulated since your household heat is not escaping. If your roof is clean or has "hot spots" you need insulation.

Thanks to government deregulation we have all sorts of opportunities to save money on telephone bills. There are a variety of telephone service choices and plans, but almost all offer discounted usage periods. Smart savers make their long distance and high unit calls during these discounted periods.

I know that for many of you this may be inconvenient, but the plan outlined in this book seeks maximum savings by reversing the convenience process. You are purposely inconveniencing yourself to save money. The savings is the start of your wealth.

AUTOMATIC SPENDING

There are some things that we spend money for that become automatic. Never questioning, never thinking, like a machine we automatically spend for these items.

Newspaper or magazine subscriptions are good examples. I'm sure when folks order these things they have great intentions of reading to keep informed. Truth is, for most people newspapers and magazines are dust collectors. They form enormous piles of trash. You'll be dollars ahead if you buy a paper or magazine on an issue by issue basis when you are really motivated to read it. You will be even more dollars ahead if you read them in your local library. Many libraries will even let you check out periodicals so you can read them at home.

Haircuts are another source of automatic purchases. Buy a haircut set and at the very least cut your kids' hair. If you have two boys, professional haircuts can cost $20 or more every three or four weeks. A haircut set costs about $15 and will save you over $200 a year. Once you get the knack you might even try cutting Dad's hair, easily doubling your annual savings.

If you're afraid you'll butcher your kids' hair, the next three or four times you take the kids to the barber carefully observe how he cuts their hair.[1] Then make your first attempt by giving trims in between visits to the barber.

I mentioned the cleaners as a possible source of savings in Chapter One. Here too is a place that we automatically spend money. Use caution when you wear clothes that require cleaning. Take off suit jackets and sweaters when you're warm. Hang your clothes up immediately after you take them off. And clean them only when they are soiled. I've saved a great deal of money by doing these simple acts.

However, some automatic spending may not be so easy to give up because it's achieved almost sacred or holy status. Take gifts. During my period of unemployment, I could not afford to buy any gifts for my family or anyone else, even for Christmas and birthdays. I felt terrible. My wife brought me to reason one day when I was feeling especially bad. She said, "What's so important about the particular day? Isn't it a day like any other day? Can't we buy a Christmas gift in July, March, or September? For that matter, why buy anything at all? Isn't it enough that we're together? Can't we celebrate in other ways?"

Beside relieving me of guilt, her words gave birth to a great savings source. From that day to the present we do not allow the calendar to dictate when we'll buy gifts. We've trained our son to wait for his Christmas presents until after Christmas when we can buy them on sale. He's learned that his patience will get him a much better present.

Same goes for birthday presents. My wife and I do not exchange birthday or anniversary gifts. When the spirit moves us and we find a good deal, we'll buy something for each other

---

[1] *I'm not trying to put barbers or hair stylists out of business; I'm just pointing out another area of potential savings.*

or ourselves. In her words, "This way we can have Christmas all year long!"

We buy gifts for friends when we find bargains, then store them. We have a closet full of small gift toys, towels, sheets, and the like. We have virtually cut out all gift-giving with adult relatives. We think it is ridiculous to spend good money buying something that will probably be returned. Nieces and nephews are different. We still buy an occasional gift for them.

Scrooges? Well, I guess that depends on how you define it. If you mean because we don't nearly kill ourselves buying gifts during the weeks preceding Christmas, I guess we qualify. However, if you mean that we don't help anyone—*you're wrong.*

We feel that the greatest gift is helping someone when they have the greatest need or are in trouble. My wife's wonderful brother ViJay was there when we needed him most. His monthly checks during my unemployment were gifts of love that can never be repaid. My wife's parents have also helped us a great deal. Recently I have had the honor to help a family member and a friend.

The same goes for charities. As we grow in wealth we feel it is our obligation to use our wealth to help others. The gifts we give each other at Christmas or birthdays can't ever equal the gifts we give out of love to others who are in need.

WASTE NOT, WANT NOT

Waste is a tremendous destroyer of wealth. Wasted food, soap, detergent, etc., is literally dollars thrown away. Visualize this the next time you pour detergent into your washer . . . see dollars instead of detergent going into your machine!

Try an experiment. Reduce the quantity of detergent that is recommended by the manufacturer. Try to find the least amount that will still do the job. Stop automatically following instructions on the back of boxes.

While you're experimenting, try a few experiments to reduce the amount of food you throw away. Because they go stale fast bakery goods are probably the foods thrown out most often. We've discovered we can reduce the amount thrown out by storing breads, pies, and cakes in the freezer. This greatly increases their shelf-life. Bread that becomes stale we freshen up by microwaving it for 15 to 20 seconds. Scraps, pieces, and crumbs we use for stuffing, bread pudding, or meat and fish coatings.

Milk that has turned sour is probably the second greatest wasted food. We turn sour milk into homemade yogurt by placing a spoonful of yogurt into a dish of sour milk, covering it with a towel or cloth, and placing it in a warm place like an unheated oven. Homemade yogurt is an excellent replacement for sour cream.

Be creative. Find ways to use leftovers. A couple of leftover chicken legs, a hand full of rice, a carrot, some peas, onion slices, and seasonings can become homemade soup. Overripe bananas can become banana bread. Grapes can be dried to raisins, etc.

Don't automatically pitch food. Think how leftovers, overripe, and stale foods can be used. If you are throwing a great deal of food away, consider buying less, making sure food containers are tightly closed, and that frequently discarded foods are used sooner. A garbage can of unused or spoiled food is a can with a silver lining.

HOW FRESH IS FRESH IS FRESH?

Our modern age has provided us with many wonderful tools for determining quality. One device is the freshness dates marked on packages. They alert us to the relative freshness of the food in the package.

Freshness dates also offer opportunities for wonderful bargains. Many products are still wholesome and reasonably fresh well beyond their freshness dates. Budget bakeries capitalize on this by selling baked goods that are near or past their freshness dates at drastically reduced prices. They also sell overstocked slow-moving lines and items whose packaging is slightly damaged. All products are of high quality, so much so that even the fussiest family member won't taste the difference.

Most bakeries are now part of large food conglomerates, and many bakeries carry extended product lines including frozen entrees and food specialties. You might pick up a frozen pizza or a microwave dinner from there also—all at a nice discount over the same products in the supermarket.

NO EASY WAY

In the past two chapters I talked about techniques that I have described as *guerilla savings*. The techniques are merely ways to save money through smart shopping and negotiating, and by developing an intolerance for loss of money. All require drive, motivation, and a degree of courage, but all begin with your willingness to try something different and ability to stick to it.

There is no easy way. If there were I would have found it, and you would be reading an entirely different book. But don't despair! *The good news is that it is still possible to become wealthy on your current income!* Persistence pays—but only when it is backed by knowledge. So read on as we move to the business elements of this program.

CHAPTER **6**

Your Annual Budget:
Blueprint for Success

For most of us our experience with budgets can be spelled in one four-letter word: P-A-I-N. Budgeting induces images of suffering, doing without the things we need or want, especially the little luxuries we reserve for ourselves. Like wood for a cozy fire on a cold winter's eve. Or a soothing hot bubble bath after a nerve-racking, day.

We've been raised with the idea that living on a budget means a humiliating, joyless life. Eat monotonous food. Wear drab clothing. Have the Saturday evening reruns as our only source of recreation. Is that what you believe, Bunky?

**HAVING A BUDGET DOESN'T MEAN YOU HAVE TO
LIVE ON MACARONI AND CHEESE**

I don't know where we got the idea that budgeting means doing without, but it's certainly widespread. Words like "scrimping" are used to describe what we believe it means to budget. Budgeting is associated with poverty. It is thought of as a last resort to keep the house and car from being repossessed.

In truth, none of this is what budgeting is all about. A budget is simply a financial plan that considers the wisest use of income sources in light of needs and obligations. By design, it forces you to project an entire year's worth of purchases and analyze them in terms of available financial resources.

Notice that this definition says nothing about how much will be spent. Nor does it say anything about scrimping and saving. In fact, unless explicitly stated otherwise, the only savings goal of a budget is to stay within the guidelines you set. It presumes that you will do whatever is necessary to accomplish that. Thus if you set a tight budget, you will need to be more frugal than if you create a more liberal budget.

The most important thing about budgeting, however, is that it is the heart of any wealth-building program. Using any of the techniques described thus far will help you, but only a budget can set your direction and keep you on target.

Budgeting and running your home like a business will be a full-time commitment for the entire family. A good way to get everyone involved is by sharing responsibilities. Jobs may be assigned and meetings can be held. Although key positions of Chief Financial Officer and Vice President of Purchasing should be held by Mom and Dad, older children can serve important roles as bookkeepers and financial analysts. And all can participate in financial planning and goal-setting sessions.

Children of all ages can be taught the value of money by asking them to help you find the best deals on items they want or need. They may be taken on shopping tours and shown how prices differ for the same items. Older children can be given responsibility for their own clothing, school, and entertainment budgets. However, care must be used to make sure they are capable of handling such a task and that they will be responsible for living within their budgets.

I told you that one of the first wealth-building decisions we made was to run our household like a business. We decided early on that our business would not be a real one unless it generated profits. We defined profits as what remains after subtracting expenses from income. Profits would be used to build assets—the foundation of wealth.

We knew that we had to build a financial plan starting with an annual budget. But how could we project expenses and income for an entire year? That was a question that bothered us—until we realized that our expense diary of monthly expenses offered us a spending history from which we could guesstimate the next year's expenses and income.

HOW TO GET STARTED

You'll need at least six months worth of expenses to make a budget and included in that six months should be periods of both high and low expenses. It would be better to have an entire year's worth of expenses to construct your budget, but it's more important to have a budget with some inaccuracies than not to have one at all.

You'll also need a pad of at least four column ledger paper, a calculator, and several sharp pencils. Budgeting does require some basic math skills. Please don't fret! Even if math has never been a strong skill for you, it is especially important you do these exercises, because they will prove to you once and for all that you can conquer anything—*including math.* Take it from me . . . remember I was the guy who couldn't balance his checkbook. I am also the guy who turned this weakness into a great strength.

Take a sheet of your ledger paper and set it up like the one illustrated in Figure 6-1[1]. Your budget worksheet will have these four columns:

Expenses — Monthly
Expenses — Annual
Budget — Annual
Budget — Monthly

---

[1] *The budget format I offer on the following pages is by no means sacrosanct. It is just one that I have found to be useful. If you feel that you can improve it, do it! And I'd appreciate it if you'd share it with me for my own edification and to help others.*

Figure 6-1: Your Budget Worksheet

Step One: Enter your fixed monthly payments in column one.

			EXPENSES MONTHLY 1990	EXPENSES ANNUAL 1990	EXPENSES ANNUAL 1991	EXPENSES MONTHLY 1991
1	FIXED	MORTGAGE/RENT				
2		PAYMENT: CAR				
3		MASTERCARD				
4	SEMI-ANNUAL	INSURANCE				
5	QUARTERLY	PROPERTY TAX				

Step Two: Multiply each fixed monthly payment by 12 and enter the results in column two.

			EXPENSES MONTHLY 1990	EXPENSES ANNUAL 1990	BUDGET ANNUAL 1991	BUDGET MONTHLY 1991
1	FIXED	MORTGAGE/RENT				
2		PAYMENT: CAR				
3		MASTERCARD				
4	SEMI-ANNUAL	INSURANCE				
5	QUARTERLY	PROPERTY TAX				

Step Three: Annualize your semi-annual or quarterly fixed payments by multiplying the payment by the number of payments you make each year and enter the results in column two.

			EXPENSES MONTHLY 1990	EXPENSES ANNUAL 1990	EXPENSES ANNUAL 1991	EXPENSES MONTHLY 1991
1	FIXED	MORTGAGE/RENT				
2		PAYMENT: CAR				
3		MASTERCARD				
4	SEMI-ANNUAL	INSURANCE				
5	QUARTERLY	PROPERTY TAX				

There are good reasons for having both monthly and annual expense totals in your budget. Monthly totals allow you to spread your expenses evenly over an entire year, thus removing severe swings in monthly expenses due to periods of high and low spending. In this way you can avoid being caught short in particularly expensive months like the winter heating season in the Midwest and also avoid the temptation to overspend during months of light expenses.

Annualizing expenses, on the other hand, helps you keep track of your standard of living and also enables you to make annual savings goals. This is important because it is very easy to allow your standard of living to grow with your income. This is particularly true if you're experiencing a period of rapid salary growth. As you make more you spend more and never seem to get ahead. Having a handle on your annual expenses lets you quickly see if this is happening to you.

Start your budget worksheet by filling in your fixed monthly expenses like mortgage or rent, car payment, and monthly payments for revolving charge accounts and other loans.[1] Enter these amounts in column one, *Expenses—Monthly*. Then annualize these expenses by multiplying each by 12 and entering them in the spaces provided in column two, *Expenses— Annual*. Next, take the fixed expenses that you pay once or twice a year, like home and car insurance, property taxes, auto licenses, and the like. Multiply each by the number of payments you make in a year and enter these in column two (see Figure 6-2).

Do the same for utilities like electric, gas or heating fuel, water, garbage, and the telephone. Write down your annual expenses in column two, then divide the expenses of each by

---

[1] *It will be a goal of your wealth-building program to eliminate revolving charges from your budget planning. With the exorbitant interest rates they charge they're wealth killers. Keep this in mind as you build your first budget.*

Figure 6-2: Getting Started

Step One: Enter your fixed monthly payments in column one.

			1 EXPENSES MONTHLY 1990	2 EXPENSES ANNUAL 1990	3	4
1	FIXED	MORTGAGE/RENT	757 43			
2		PAYMENT: CAR	247 45			
3		MASTERCARD	220 48			
4	SEMI-ANNUAL	INSURANCE				
5	QUARTERLY	PROPERTY TAX				

Step Two: Multiply each fixed monthly payment by 12 and enter the results in column two. (Example: Monthly mortgage payment is $757.43 x 12 = $9,089.16)

			1 EXPENSES MONTHLY 1990	2 EXPENSES ANNUAL 1990	3	4
1	FIXED	MORTGAGE/RENT	757 43	9089 16		
2		PAYMENT: CAR	247 45	2969 40		
3		MASTERCARD	220 48	2645 76		
4	SEMI-ANNUAL	INSURANCE		1065 00		
5	QUARTERLY	PROPERTY TAX		2250 00		

Step Three: Annualize your semi-annual or quarterly fixed payments by multiplying the payment by the number of payments you make each year and enter the results in column two. (Example: Quarterly insurance payments are $266.25 x 4 payments = $1,065.00)

			1 EXPENSES MONTHLY 1990	2 EXPENSES ANNUAL 1990	3	4
1		MORTGAGE/RENT	757 43	9089 16		
2		PAYMENT: CAR	247 45	2969 40		
3		MASTERCARD	220 48	2645 76		
4		INSURANCE		1065 00		
5		PROPERTY TAX		2250 00		

12 and enter them in column one. If you don't have a year's worth of utility expenses you can get previous year totals from your utility companies. Sometimes you can get several years' expenditures, allowing you to calculate your average expenses for the past three to five years by adding the total of each year and dividing by the total number of years (see Figure 6-3).

Returning to your budget work sheet, next analyze expenses that are easily pooled like gas for the car, commuting expenses (bus or train fares, parking fees), groceries, cleaning bills, medical/dental expenses, money spent to eat out, etc. Total all expenses made during the past year for each category. Again enter annual totals for each and divide them by 12 to arrive at an average monthly expense.

If you only have six, seven, or eight months of expenses, you'll need to guesstimate your annual expenses. To do this, total each category of expenses and then guesstimate what you believe your expenses will be for the remaining months of the year. To this total add 10%[1]. Then divide each by 12 and enter your figures in column one (see Figure 6-4).

The last group of expenses will take a little detective work. Refer to your expense diary and attempt to group common expenses for home repairs and supplies, lawn and garden, automobile repairs and maintenance, clothing for each member of the family, school expenses, music lessons and team sport fees, and entertainment. Carefully think about what should be included in each category. For your future reference, write what expenses have been included in each category on a separate sheet. For example, clothing should include shoes, socks, underwear, slacks, shirts, blouses, dresses, suits, coats,

---

[1] *The reason I want you to add 10% is because we all have a tendency to underestimate expenses and overestimate income. It's human nature. If you do the reverse, you may end up with a nice unexpected bonus at the end of the year instead of a loss.*

Figure 6-3: Getting a Handle on Utility Expenses

Total your utility expenses for the year and enter them in column two.
Divide each sum by twelve and enter the answers in column one.

				1 EXPENSES MONTHLY 1990	2 EXPENSES ANNUAL 1990
1			MORTGAGE/RENT	757 43	9089 16
2			PAYMENT: CAR	247 45	2969 40
3			MASTERCARD	220 48	2645 76
4			INSURANCE	—	1065 60
5			PROPERTY TAX	—	2250 00
6			✓HEAT	44 14	529 68
7			✓ELECTRIC	41 79	501 48
8			✓TELEPHONE	57 42	689 04
9			✓WATER/GARBAGE	182 4	2188 80

If you can get previous years' totals from your utility companies, follow
these steps to obtain monthly and yearly average costs for each service.

Step One: Add the totals for each year.

1990	$529.68
1989	448.38
1988	407.88
1987	413.17
1986	475.49
Total	$2,274.60

Step Two: Divide your answer by the number of years worth of expenses
and enter your result in column two.

$2,274.60 ÷ 5 years = $454.92 per year average

Step Three: Divide this yearly average by 12 and enter the result in
column one.

$454.92 ÷ 12 months = $37.91 per month average

Figure 6-4: Guesstimating Annual Expenses

Step One: Total each expense category for the months you have.

	Eat Out	Groceries	Auto Gas	Med/Dental
January	$43.45	$216.65	$82.55	$ —
February	36.75	190.60	70.95	88.69
March	45.85	154.30	83.80	—
April	16.53	171.90	91.75	—
May	33.00	221.35	64.95	—
June	58.30	193.14	75.80	25.60
Total	$233.88	$1,147.94	$469.80	$114.29

Step Two: Guesstimate your expenses for the remainder of the year and add 10% to each total. Enter this amount in column two of your ledger.

	Jan to June (Actual)	July to Dec (Guess)	Subtotal	+	10%	Total for Year
Eat Out	$ 233.38	+ 250.00	= 483.38	+	48.34	= $ 531.72
Groceries	1,147.94	+ 1,300.00	= 2,447.94	+	244.79	= 2,692.73
Auto Gas	469.80	+ 500.00	= 969.80	+	96.98	= 1,066.78
Med/Dental	114.29	+ 400.00	= 514.29	+	51.43	= 565.72

Step Three: Divide each by 12 and enter your result in column one.

Eat Out	$ 531.72	+	12 months	=	$ 44.31 per month
Groceries	2,692.73	+	12 months	=	224.39 per month
Auto Gas	1,066.78	+	12 months	=	88.90 per month
Med/Dental	565.72	+	12 months	=	47.14 per month

---

jackets, and hats, etc., for each family member. Home repairs should include tools, supplies, and professional service charges for regular home maintenance. That would include paint, brushes, drain cleaner, nails, lumber, turpentine, furnace filters, soft water salt, annual furnace and air-conditioning service, and repairs for washer and dryer (see Figure 6-5).

Items that do not fit any category or are purchased infrequently may be itemized under miscellaneous, but don't let this category become too big. It should consist of less than a dozen or so items. If it is bigger than this you need to analyze your

---

Figure 6-5: Grouping Common Expenses

Household Supplies

Laundry supplies	$ 55.90
Floor wax, furniture polish	22.45
Toilet paper, tissues	38.90
Film, photo-developing	37.50
Personal: toothpaste, shave cream	64.35
Drain openers, cleaners, etc.	21.65
Total	$ 240.75

---

miscellaneous expenses to determine if they belong in categories you've already constructed or in new ones.

Apartment dwellers: You may not have all the expenses that have been listed, but you still need to allow for certain maintenance and household supplies like: floor wax, carpet cleaning supplies, drain openers, detergent, money for laundromat, bathroom cleaners, etc.

Remember the object of budgeting is to be as complete as possible in your analysis. Therefore, if you have expenses that do not fit the categories I have provided . . . make up new ones. Try to pool common expenses into common groups.

TRANSLATING THE PAST INTO THE FUTURE

You are now ready to start formulating your first budget. You begin by reviewing the expenses you have itemized in the first two columns of your worksheet.

Once again, start with your fixed expenses. If you will be living in the same house and owning the same car, the first part of your budget is easy. Just transfer your figures for these items from columns one and two to columns three and four. However, if you are considering a new home or car, you'll need to complete your entire budget before you enter any figures. The reason is that you must first assess whether or not you can afford an increased payment. (Never mind how much your realtor says you can qualify for in terms of a mortgage. These figures are based on the maximum indebtedness a bank will allow for a person in your financial position. These figures do not take into account future needs nor savings. They are the outer limits of affordability.) For now just plug in your current payments. After you complete your budget you can subtract your total projected expenses from your expected income to ascertain your profit outlook. At that time you can decide how much of your profits you'd like to allocate for an increased payment[1].

Move on to annual or semi-annual fixed expenses. Again, if you are contemplating a new home or car you will need to return to this portion of your budget if you decide to proceed with a purchase to make allowances for increases in this expense category. For now transfer your figures from columns one and two to three and four (see Figure 6-6).

Review your utility bills for the past year. Consider what you can do to reduce expenses. The telephone bill is an easy place to start. How much was spent for long distance calls last year? Can you cut your long distance in half or more? If so, reduce your telephone expenses by that amount. Then set some telephone policies. First, all long distance calls must be made during discounted periods. (Check your telephone company for times.) Second, local calls will be held to a minimum.

---

[1] *To be precise, if you are considering the purchase of a new home you need to consider how much of the increase in your payment will be offset by tax breaks. A way to get a rough estimate is to use your last year's tax form. Plug in your current income and figure your taxes both with your current payment and your new projected payment. Subtract the difference in taxes and divide that figure by 12. Last subtract the result from your projected new payment to get your net after tax payment.*

Figure 6-6: Translating the Past into the Future

Transfer your figures for your fixed payments from columns one and two to columns three and four as is, even if you're considering the purchase of a new home or car. Reason? By completing your entire budget using your present payments first, you'll be in a better position to determine how much more of a payment you can comfortably afford.

			1 EXPENSES MONTHLY 1990	2 EXPENSES ANNUAL 1990	3 BUDGET ANNUAL 1991	4 BUDGET MONTHLY 1991
1		MORTGAGE/RENT	75743	908916	908916	75743
2		PAYMENT: CAR	24745	296940	296940	24745
3		MASTERCARD	22048	264576	250000	20833
4		INSURANCE	—	106500	106500	8875
5		PROPERTY TAX	—	225000	225000	18750

Set goals for other utilities as well. Winter daytime temperatures can be held at 70°F and night-time temperatures at 65°F. Summer use of air-conditioning will be restricted to the hottest days of the season. Or lawns will be watered at night only and monitored so water is not wasted. Showers will be held to seven minutes at low pressure. It will be hard to estimate the effect of these new policies, so for this year use the same expense you had in columns one and two for your budget figures in columns three and four. Next year scrutinize your utility expenses to determine the effectiveness of your new policies and adjust your budget accordingly.

The next category of expenses you can really set some goals for (see Figure 6-7). Using the guerilla savings techniques outlined in Chapter Four, you should be able to reduce your expenses for groceries, cleaning bills, and household supplies by at least 35%. For budget purposes this year start with a modest goal of 20%: Subtract 20% from the expenses listed in column two

Figure 6-7: Applying Guerilla Savings

Since you'll be applying guerilla savings techniques, you can reduce certain expenses. For your first budget try reducing your annual grocery, household supply, and cleaners budgets by at least 20%. Cut your eating-out, entertainment, and babysitting budget by 50%. Write these figures down in column three (Budget—Annual). Then divide each by 12 to arrive at your monthly budget figures for column four. (The babysitting money I'm referring to is the amount spent for entertainment. If you need a sitter to work, you obviously can't cut your budget without affecting your earning power.)

			1 EXPENSES MONTHLY 1990	2 EXPENSES ANNUAL 1990	3 BUDGET ANNUAL 1991	4 BUDGET MONTHLY 1991
1		MORTGAGE/RENT	757 43	9089 16	9089 16	757 43
2		PAYMENT: CAR	247 45	2969 40	2969 40	247 45
3		MASTERCARD	220 48	2645 76	2500 00	208 33
4		INSURANCE	—	1065 00	1065 00	88 75
5		PROPERTY TAX	—	2250 00	2250 00	187 50
6		HEAT	44 14	529 68	529 68	44 14
7		ELECTRIC	41 79	501 48	501 48	41 79
8		TELEPHONE	57 42	689 04	689 04	57 42
9		WATER/GARBAGE	18 24	218 88	218 88	18 24
10		GROCERIES	161 54	1938 50 -20%	1550 80	129 23
11		AUTO GAS	68 10	817 20 -20%	653 76	54 48
12		HOUSEHOLD SUPPLIES	20 06	240 75 -20%	192 60	16 05
13		CLEANERS	11 31	135 66 -20%	108 53	9 05
14		EAT OUT	41 21	494 52 -50%	247 26	20 61
15		ENTERTAINMENT	57 08	685 00 -50%	342 50	28 54
16		BABYSITTING	22 08	265 00 -50%	132 50	11 04

and record the resulting number in columns three and four. Cut by 50% the expenses for eating out, entertaining, and non-essential baby-sitting and enter the amounts in your budget columns (see Figure 6-7).

The remaining budget items will take a bit more analysis. Consider your household's overall needs. For example, does the house need painting this year? How much grass seed and fertilizer is needed for the garden? What kind of car repairs are you facing based upon your current annual mileage? Do you expect any additional medical or dental bills beyond what you spent last year? And so forth. On a separate sheet write down what you have included in your projection. Review your expenses for the past year. Consider your needs for the coming year and arrive at a projected cost. Write down these figures in your budget columns three and four (Figure 6-8).

Next think about each family members' needs for the coming year. Survey them about what they believe they'll need. Ask them to make lists of needs and wants. Encourage them to be as precise as possible. Tell them that you'll attempt to give them as many wants as possible, but you'll need to have their wants listed in priority so they get the things they value most. Be brutally honest in your evaluation.

Review each total listed in column two and consider the costs in light of your family's needs for the coming year. If you spent more last year than you have projected for the coming year, review your expense diary to determine the kinds of items you purchased. This will help you to determine whether your projections are accurate. Carefully analyze your expenses. Did you buy enough dresses for yourself and shirts for Dad to carry you through this year, or will you need more? Adjust your clothing budgets for each family member until you are confident in your projections. Then enter your total budget figure in column three, *Budget—Annual.* Next divide each by 12 and enter in column four, *Budget—Monthly* (see Figure 6-9).

Figure 6-8: Needs for the Coming Year

Analyze your needs for the coming year by budget category:

Home Repairs

Paint bedrooms	
6 gallons of paint	$ 48.00
brushes, rollers	10.00
AC/furnace service	75.00
Furnace filters	12.00
Repair fence	
lumber, nails, paint	125.00
Repair sidewalk cracks	85.00
Miscellaneous	50.00
Total	$ 405.00

Auto Maintenance

Assumption: I expect to put 12,000 miles on car, bringing it to the 48,000 mile level.

Three oil changes @ $21.00 each	$ 63.00
Brake job (pads/turn rotors)	350.00
Tune-up	75.00
Total	$ 488.00

Garden

Grass, flower seeds/plants	$ 25.00
Fertilizer (six bags)	35.00
Garden tools (spade, rakes, hoe)	40.00
Gas/oil for mower/snow thrower	15.00
Miscellaneous	20.00
Total	$ 135.00

Don't be discouraged if you find this difficult at first. This is a tough job, one that requires time and effort. Decide that you will be as accurate as possible. Make a game of it. See how close you can come. Your efforts will be well worth it, because for the first time in your life you'll know exactly how and where your money is spent and how you can control your financial future.

Continue category by category in the same way. Take the expenses in column two and add or subtract expenses based on needs for the coming year. Be thorough and exacting. Don't allow any expenses to escape your projection.

After you've translated each expense category, look at your entire budget. Have you detailed all your family expenses? You may find it necessary to add a few new categories. Tailor your budget to your family's needs and interests, but remember the goal of this exercise is to provide a plan for wealth, so don't create new expense categories just to have them.

At the bottom of the sheet add categories that occur infrequently. Examples include furniture and appliances. Instead of calculating past expenses for these items, you're going to do some pure projection. For instance, you may foresee a need for a new refrigerator in the next three years. To be sure you'll have the money you'll need to buy it then, you must budget for it now. Calculate the cost of the kind of refrigerator you'll want, divide that cost by three, and enter that amount in column three. In like manner consider other periodic expenses. If you intend to purchase an item during the coming year, then project the full amount. For other items you'll need to project the portion you need to save this year. For example, purchases that will need to be made five years from now require you to budget one-fifth or 20% of the estimated future purchase price. Finally divide these items by 12 and enter them in column four.

A final budget category should be reserved for an emergency fund. Take the most expensive appliance or piece of equipment you own, like a furnace. Determine how many years of life it has left. Calculate its replacement cost and divide it by the number of years until replacement. This will give you a cushion that can be used for any emergency (see Figure 6-10).

Figure 6-9: Surveying Family Member Needs

	Needs 1991	Expenses 1990	Budget 1991
Mom			
2 pair of shoes	$ 70.00		
10 pair of nylons	19.90		
3 dresses	120.00		
1 pair of slacks	20.00		
Total Mom	$229.90	$343.23	$300.00
Dad			
1 pair of shoes	$ 50.00		
6 pair of underwear	7.00		
1 suit	235.00		
1 jacket	45.00		
1 pair of gloves	5.00		
Total Dad	$342.00	$1,019.50	$450.00
Junior			
2 pair of shoes	$ 50.00		
4 slacks	70.00		
5 shirts	60.00		
Total Junior	$180.00	$65.45	$275.00

			1	2	3	4
			EXPENSES MONTHLY 1990	EXPENSES ANNUAL 1990	BUDGET ANNUAL 1991	BUDGET MONTHLY 1991
17		CLOTHING (MOM)		34323	300 00	25 00
18		CLOTHING (DAD)		101950	450 00	3750
19		CLOTHING (CHILD)		6545	275 00	2292

PROFITS P-L-E-A-S-E . . .

Now comes the moment of truth! At the very bottom of the sheet record all your sources of income for the coming year: Net (after taxes) salary, gifts, bonuses and commissions, interest and dividends, tax refunds, etc. Make sure your salary projection

---

Figure 6-10: Budgeting for Emergencies

Emergencies come when you are least able to pay for them. That's why it is helpful to prepare for them ahead of time. Do this by estimating the cost of your most expensive appliance replacement or repair item (a new furnace or roof?). Decide how many years before it will need to be replace or repaired. Estimate the replacement or repair cost and divide it by the number of years until your predicted replacement date. Enter the result in column three. Divide this figure by 12 and enter the answer in column four.

Example: New furnace cost $1,000
                Present furnace good for 8 years

$1,000 ÷ 8 years = $125 per year *(enter in column three)*
$125 ÷ 12 months = $10.42 per month *(enter in column four)*

				1 EXPENSES MONTHLY 1990	2 EXPENSES ANNUAL 1990	3 BUDGET ANNUAL 1991	4 BUDGET MONTHLY 1991
20		NEW REFRIG (1994) $750			÷3	250 00	20 83
21		NEW TV (1996) $525			÷5	105 00	8 75
22		EMER-FURNACE (1998) $1,000			÷8	125 00	10 42

---

includes your annual raise, and make sure you state your salary in net-after-tax terms. Your gross salary may look good, but it's meaningless in terms of savings. Last, if you expect a tax refund add this amount to the bottom of the sheet (see Figure 6-11).

Add up your budgeted expenses and put the total in the space provided. Add up your income. Subtract your expenses from your income. Do you have a profit? If you do, divide the profit by your total income and multiply by 100 to calculate your profit percentage (see Figure 6-12).

If you project a profit of 10% to 15%, you're off to a good start. In later years you'll want to increase your profit percentage. You'll be able to accomplish this through better control of expenses and by earnings on investments. For a point of comparison, at the Trout household, our annual goal is a minimum profit of 35%. In good years we've earned profits of 50% or more!

If you have a profit, you are also in a position to consider the purchase of a new home or car with a portion of the profit. But don't be tempted to spend your entire profit. If you do, you'll defeat the purpose of budgeting.

If you have a deficit or a profit of less than 10%, you'll need to readjust your budget. The first thing you can forget about is making any new, large purchases this year. A marginal profit level or a deficit indicates that you're at or beyond your ability to live on your present income. Therefore you must find ways to handle your present expenses before you can consider anything else!

If you're in this position, it's time for your first series of budget cuts. Even if you have a profit of 15%, you may want to

---

Figure 6-11: The Moment of Truth

Total your expenses for column three. Next enter all sources of annual *net* income (salary, interest income, tax refunds) at the bottom of your ledger. Subtract your total projected net income from your projected budget expenses.

How much do you have left?

22		EMER-FURNACE (1998) $1,000			−8	125 00	1042
23		TOTAL BUDGET EXPENSE:	24545.59				
24		DAD SALARY	24682.33				
25		MOM P.T. JOB	3785.45				
26		TAX REFUND	850.00				
27		GIFTS	150.00				
28		TOTAL ANNUAL INCOME (NET)	29467.78				
29		(LESS BUDGETED EXPENSES)	24545.59				
30		BALANCE (PROFIT?)	4922.19				

Figure 6-12: Calculating Your Potential Profits

If you have a balance remaining after you subtract your projected budget expenses, congratulations! You're on the road to profits and wealth.

The next question is how much of a profit will you earn?

To calculate your potential profit for the coming year, divide your balance by your total porjected income and multiply the answer by 100.

$$\$4,922.19 \div 29,467.78 = .1670$$
$$.1670 \times 100 = 16.70\% \text{ or } 16.7\%$$

---

look for ways to increase your profit margin. Businesses go through this exercise every year as a routine part of the budget process. You should consider it the same way.

Look first for easy adjustments, things that you can reduce or eliminate without creating undue hardship. Look first at what you have budgeted for eating out. Cut it in half again. Next move to your utilities budget. Cut long distance calls to the barest minimum, and reduce your lighting. Can you cut your auto mileage? How much will this save in terms of gas and service costs? Look at what you have allowed for vacations and entertainment. Can this budget be reduced?

Adjust your budget and retotal your expenses. Subtract your adjusted total expenses from your income to see where you stand now. If you still have a deficit or have not attained a 10% profit you must return to your budget for further adjustments.

Next move to your clothing budget. Eliminate all wants and carefully scrutinize your needs to make sure that everything that has been included is truly a need. Perhaps a pair of shoes or another clothing item can be deducted from each family member's allocation. Or perhaps you can wait for that new suit.

Move on to your home maintenance and repair budget and to your garden budget. Are there some things that can be postponed? Also look at your budget for projected future purchases. Are all the items necessary or can some be eliminated? Or can they be postponed from budgeting for a year or projected over a longer time frame? If so, readjust these budgets and again add up your budgeted expenses and subtract them from your income.

If after these adjustments you still haven't achieved a 10% profit, more serious adjustments must be made, like eliminating eating out, outside entertainment, and vacations. Or taking all wants out of the clothing budget and reducing or eliminating all gifts[1]. (Please no moaning or whining.) If you have not achieved a 10% profit after this stage you have a serious budget problem, one that is probably linked to your past spending. Examine the amount you have budgeted for revolving charge payments or personal loans. Divide this amount by your total income and multiply it by 100. What does this equal . . . 5%, 10%, 15%, or more? Revolving charge payments are profits going down the drain. Make it your goal to use your profits this year to eliminate your revolving charge balances as soon as possible. Take the first action today by cutting your cards up today.

If you cannot eliminate your budget deficit after the first two series of budget adjustments, you may be facing a potential financial crisis. To avoid it you must seek an immediate solution. Turn to Chapter 10, "Survival Solutions for Credit Kamikazes," before reading further. Then return to this chapter and complete the book.

---

[1] *You'll notice that I did not cut the grocery budget even at this stage of budget cuts. Having nourishing, tasty food is basic to survival. If you can reduce expenses further by taking advantage of special sales that's great, but don't cut the quality or quantity of your food just to save money. Good food keeps the family morale high even during tough times.*

Beyond the Numbers

After you have worked the numbers, you'll have constructed your first working budget, but your planning is not complete until you set some budget and financial goals for the year. We find it helpful at this time to also include some non-financial goals like personal development and family welfare. Our goals include the following:

1. Earnings goal in terms of wages.
2. Savings goal in dollars.
3. Rate of return (i.e., 7%, 8%) expected from investments.
4. Investments for further or ongoing investigation.
5. Career goals.
6. Personal development goals.
7. Health and fitness goals.
8. Spiritual goals.

As a final part of the annual budget exercise we find it helpful to conduct a net worth analysis. This analysis helps us to discern our precise financial position and establishes a benchmark to assess our progress toward becoming wealthy. I have provided a form for you to conduct your own net worth analysis (see Figure 6-13).

KEEPING TRACK TO STAY ON TRACK

A budget can do nothing to help you create wealth unless it is used. You use it by comparing your budget figures with your Expense Diary each month. The process starts by first totalling your monthly expenses and subtracting them from the income you earned that month.

Compare the resulting total profit with the one you projected in your budget. Look back over the last several months. Are you on target? If you have exceeded your profit projection, don't decide to increase expenses. You may need this cushion to balance out some unexpected expenses in future months. If you have fallen short of your target, you may need to make adjustments. Perhaps you underestimated some costs, or perhaps prices have gone up. In either case you will need to adjust your budget.

To stay within budget, each budget increase must be balanced with a corresponding budget cut. (I know that these things can be frustrating, but instead of feeling down, think of these times as opportunities to stay in control of your finances. With money management as with everything else in life, *it's not what happens to you that's important but how you react to it!*)

Being off target isn't the only reason you may want to adjust your budget. Perhaps you've found a once-in-a-lifetime buy on that refrigerator you planned to purchase three years from now. The new box is going for 35% of its retail price. It's too good to pass up, but it's not in your budget. What do you do? The answer: To stay in budget, you must transfer budget money earmarked for other items to make up for this unbudgeted purchase. That may mean a vacation at home this year instead of a cabin in Wisconsin. Or no new couch.

Yes, Betty, Frank is going to gripe about not being able to go on his favorite fishing trip to Canada! And I know, Bill, Sue's going to raise Cain about eliminating her aerobics classes! That's the breaks! If you truly want to become wealthy on your current income, you will have to make some sacrifices in your lifestyle. After all, if your lifestyle was so great in the first place you wouldn't have bought this book. Going for the gold when you weren't born with the golden spoon takes some prospecting. You can't strike pay dirt if you're not willing to sometimes eat beans and work long and hard.

Figure 6-13: How to Figure Your Net Worth

Fill in the blanks. Then add the amounts entered in *what you own* and substract the amounts entered in *what you owe* to get your net worth.

Assets (what you own)

_____ Cash—checking accounts, savings accounts, certificates of deposit.

_____ Securities—stocks, bonds, municipal funds (current value).

_____ IRAs, vested portions of retirement programs, profit sharing.

_____ Real Estate—equity in home, condo, cottage (market value).

_____ Autos, boats, airplanes—(market value).

_____ Gold, silver, gemstones, coins, jewelry—(appraised value or ounce rate for precious metals and 40% of current retail value for jewelry).

_____ Valuables—art, oriental rungs, antiques, furs (appraised value or 40% of current retail price).

_____ Collections—stamps, coins, train sets, spoons, plates, etc. (appraised value or collector catalogue price).

_____ Cash value of life insurance, annuities.

_____ Redeemable deposits, pledged savings accounts.

_____ Furniture and appliances—(price paid less 60%).

_____ **Total assets**

Liabilities (what you owe)

_____ Balance remaining on mortage(s).

_____ Balance remaining on auto loans.

_____ Amount owed on credit cards/personal loans.

_____ **Total liabilities**

Net Worth (total assets – total liabilities)

$_____ total net worth as of _____.

                                          (Date)

Probably the most important thing in a wealth-building strategy is consistency of purpose. You must create a plan and discipline yourself to use it. It's critical that you reserve time each month for budget duties. A monthly analysis is essential to successful budgeting. To accomplish this you must keep an accurate account of daily expenses in your Expense Diary.

Learning How To Pay Your Bills

What's to learn? You write a check and that's that! Right? Wrong! If we are going to run our homes like a business, we should pay our bills like a business would. And the first thing to learn is that businesses don't pay when they're billed. They hold bills for 30, 60, or even 90 days or longer. Accountants call this *float.* Float allows your money to earn the maximum amount of interest before you are penalized for not paying the bill on time.

Commercial businesses have more time available to float bills than we do as individuals, but we can use the float too. Nearly every bill has a cutoff date after which a penalty is assessed. Usually it's 25 to 30 days past the payment due date. Knowing this, you can arrange your bills for payment by due date. Obviously early-due dates get paid first. If you can pay your bill in person without making a special trip, you can increase your float by paying it one day before the cut off. If you must mail it, allow five to sevens days.

A year's worth of float can earn you $100 or more in earned interest—provided, of course, that you keep your money in an interest-bearing account like a money market account. Think of that . . . $100 or more of net income just by taking greater care of how you pay your bills.

Another payment decision you'll need to make is when to pay cash and when to use credit. I mentioned in an earlier chapter how my wife got a great deal on shirts by offering to pay cash. You should try this too. We've found that some merchants may even agree to split the merchant fee assessed them by charge card companies if you agree not to use a card. This is particularly true when what you are buying will cost purchases costing hundreds or thousands of dollars. To pull it off, however, you will need to deal with either the store owner or the general manager. A cashier won't be able to help you.

What can you expect to get? A merchant is charged 2% to 3% by the charge card company every time a card is used. If you ask them to split the merchant fee if you pay cash, you can expect a 1% to 1.5% discount for using cash; on a thousand-dollar sale, 1.5% is $15.00. If merchants argue with you, tell them you're losing interest by paying cash. If they refuse to deal, pay with a credit card and pay the bill before the card assesses you a finance charge. Depending on where you fall on the billing cycle, you'll have anywhere from 30 to 50 days before the charge will be payable. The float alone will earn you in interest anywhere from $6.18 to $15.45 in earned interest at 7.25%.

A smart merchant will grab your offer. He's dollars ahead. He doesn't have to reduce the profitability of his sale by the merchant fee; more important, he doesn't have to wait to be paid by the credit card company, which can take months. But no matter how he reacts you'll be ahead through the proper use of credit and float.

SOMETIMES IT'S BETTER TO BORROW

I went to great lengths at the start of this book to explain how much trouble you can get into through the misuse of credit. Well, the converse is also true. Through the *proper* use of credit you can achieve a great many financial advantages. However, you must carefully think through each situation before you use credit, no matter how good the deal sounds.

Some credit cards actually pay you to use them! I have a VISA® card that pays me in cold cash for using it. The terms of this card are that for amounts charged to the card exceeding $150 I will be credited 0.5% if I pay the full balance within 25 days after the billing date. That means, on charges totalling $5,000 I will be paid $24.25 for using the card. Imagine that . . . having a credit card company pay you to use their card! You can have this same privilege too! This VISA® card is issued by Beverly Bank in Oak Lawn Illinois. (You may write or call them for information at: Credit Card Information, Beverly Bank, 10312 S. Cicero, Oak Lawn, IL 60453, 708-499-7600.)

As your cash hoard grows, you'll discover that bankers will suddenly become interested in you. You'll start to receive all kinds of offers for loans and credit cards. Best yet, you'll find yourself in the position to obtain some very lucrative credit opportunities.

For example, last spring I was searching for some bargain interest rates for a car loan. I called a number of bankers and explained I had sufficient cash to buy the car outright but didn't want to lose the earnings the cash provided. A couple of bankers offered me the opportunity to buy the car, and at the same time keep the cash, the car and title, and the interest.

How? Instead of buying the car, I would buy a certificate of deposit for the amount I wished to borrow and the length of time I wanted. I would borrow against the CD for 2% more than the interest the CD paid. The 2% the bank would keep as their loan transaction fee. I would use the cash from the CD to buy the car and obtain the car and the title. My monthly payments would be used to buy back the CD Therefore at the end of the note I would have not only the car, but also the principal and interest from the loan.

I didn't take up this offer, because I found another more attractive offer for 2.9% more interest that allowed me to keep more of my money in my own portfolio. Here's how this deal works. Beverly Bank which was mentioned earlier has a low, low car loan program that allowed me to borrow $18,000 for five years at 4.9% simple interest. To qualify, I had to open a non-interest-bearing checking account and maintain a minimum balance of $6,000. The checking account carries no service charge, so the only fee I pay is the interest. I chose this program over the CD ones because it allows me greater investment flexibility and higher potential earnings on the remaining $12,000.

Where were they when I needed them? In my credit-card-junkie period I paid through the nose for car loans. Why couldn't I find deals like that then? The reason banks are willing to offer these kind of programs to folks like I am now is that we offer them less risk. Each year thousands of cars, boats, and homes are repossessed because the owners are unable to meet their loan and mortgage obligations. Repossessions are losses not only to the car and home owners; they also represent tremendous losses to lenders, because the repossessed cars and homes are usually sold below the cost of the loan. The only people who make out in these deals are the buyers of the repossessed items. Typically they're folks who have large amounts of cash.

Following a strict budget that consistently produces profits is the way to develop your cash hoard. However, it is just as important that you plow those profits back into your business by investing in income-producing investments and allowing them to compound.

BUDGETING IS NO FUN . . . OR IS IT?

A close friend of mine read this chapter and told me that I should change it, because it wasn't as much fun as the earlier chapters. I thought about what he had to say but couldn't figure how I could frame the material in a light or humorous way. The more I thought about it, the more I realized that the real fun in budgeting is seeing the progress of your efforts. If you've never been able to save much more than a few dollars, you'll be thrilled when you have put away $1,000. I know. I've been there. And let me tell you that the thrill magnifies exponentially when you break through $10,000!

At that point the interest alone becomes significant. Each month you'll watch your money grow by $70 to $100, and you'll know that even if you don't save another dime, within ten years or less your money will grow to $20,000 just from the interest compounding. That's exciting. I can also guarantee, however, that you won't stop saving once you reach $10,000. No, that level of money will be the impetus for greater savings and within ten years you may have $100,000 or more!

Now that's what I call *real* fun!

CHAPTER **7**

Long-Range Planning:
When You Wish Upon a Star

Somewhere beyond wishing, hoping, dreaming, and cold calculated scheming lies a realm of positive expectancy, a state of mind, method, and action available for the wealth-seeker to use to make his dreams come true. In its physical form, it's a long-range plan complete with annual goals. Metaphysically, it's your faith in your ability to achieve your plan's lofty objectives.

Relax. You don't think that I'm going to give you a sermon or a discussion of some curious metaphysical approach to wealth after I've spent a hundred or so pages laying out a practical plan, do you? No. What I hope to help you realize is that planning combined with imagination, belief, and wish power lets you reach your own higher states of consciousness, states you seldom use, but ones that can help you to realize great success. Let me illustrate. . . .

WHY DIDN'T I THINK OF THAT?

It amazes me how people come up with profitable new solutions to relatively simple problems. You know how it goes. All your life you've been working on something, experiencing daily frustration struggling with some small part of your task. Then some schmoe turns your small struggle into a multi-million-dollar product and you lament, "Why didn't I think of that?"

It happens to all of us at one time or another. Ingenious solutions to mischievous problems escape us, only to be discovered by others who see the opportunity instead of difficulty. The reason we can't see it is that we become so caught up with our task or struggle we become unable to see the forest for the trees. The same thing can happen to us in a wealth-building program if we don't look at the big picture.

For example, we may be so driven to save money that when the biggest opportunity of our lifetime comes along, we may actually refuse to invest in it. A long-range plan not only gives us success targets, it opens our minds to what may be possible. It allows us to use greater mental powers. When an opportunity presents itself we will be unconsciously drawn to it.

TAKING THE LONG VIEW

In Chapter Six I suggested that you consider setting annual financial and non-financial goals after you have prepared your annual budget. These goals give your budget a sense of purpose and direction.

You're now going to do the same type of thing for the next five years. I like using a five-year time period for two reasons:

1. Five years is the planning period typically used by businesses. If I want to run my home like a business, a five-year plan represents another tool we can use to help keep us in a business-like atmosphere.
2. Five years is too long for precise mathematical planning, so it forces us to do some creative brain-storming, with time for wonderment and even a little reckless imagineering. Five years is also ample time for miracles to happen.

The physical plan involves a visionary blending of strategy, dreams, and faith. It can progress from concrete and factual to abstract and fanciful, or from known and owned to unknown and wished-for.

In Figure 7-1 (pages 122 and 123), I offer a sample planning format you can use. In it you can project your income and net worth for the next five years and envision how you'll achieve it. Please don't be overwhelmed by the format. I felt compelled to provide as complete a wealth-building program for you as possible. This meant offering you from the start advanced concepts for which you may not be ready.

Another problem I faced when I constructed this planner was having to translate into words thought processes that are habitual for me, processes that are now based upon years of investing experience. For example, it is relatively easy for me to project expected returns for various assets including real estate. The reason is that investing is a regular part of my life and I keep current on rates of return through a variety of sources.

When you attempt your first plan, you will not have the same base of experience to draw upon, so your first attempt may contain a large margin of error. That's okay. Although I spent nearly a year in the library doing research on investing before I produced my first five-year plan, it too contained many errors. Indeed, during my first year of actual investing I had to rewrite my plan twice to make it workable.

That's the way it should be. Planning is an evolving, dynamic process. Your plan will grow with your knowledge and experience and will need to be refined and rewritten to reflect changes in investment conditions and economic circumstances. Flexibility is the key word in planning as in all wealth-producing activities.

However, to plan you will need some guidelines on what are reasonable rates of return for basic investments. These are

Figure 7-1: The Next-Five Planner

(Plan Period: 19_____ to 19_____)

	19___	19___	19___	19___	19___
I. Income Assets					
A. Net Earnings					
(1) Primary job					
(2)					
(3)					
B. Interest/Dividends					
C. Rent/Business Inc					
Total Income (A–C)					
II. Other Assets					
A. Securities					
B. IRAs/Vested Pensions					
C. Real Estate					
D. Autos/Boats/Planes					
E. Gold/Jewelry					
F. Valuables/Collections					
G. Insurance-Cash Value					
H. Redeemable Deposits					
I. Furniture/Miscellaneous					
Total Other Assets (A–I)					

Figure 7-1: The Next-Five Planner, *Cont'd*

(Plan Period: 19_____ to 19_____)

	19___	19___	19___	19___	19___
III. Cash					
A. Checking Accounts					
B. Money Markets/CDs					
Total Cash					
IV. Liabilities					
A. Mortgage(s)					
B. Auto Loans					
C. Credit Cards					
D. Other					
Total Liabilites					
V. NET WORTH (I+II+III–IV)					
SAVINGS GOAL (% of Net Income)					

Goals:

19_____ _____
19_____ _____
19_____ _____
19_____ _____
19_____ _____

provided for you in Chapter Eight on investing basics. What I suggest you do is read the rest of the book before you attempt to construct your first investment plan. Then just rough something out.

At the end of your first year of recording daily expenses and researching investments, you can return to your five-year plan and refine or redo it. But do commit something to paper now. There's some magic in this first little game of What If. The magic will motivate and propel you forward.

To help you I've prepared a sample five-year plan in Figure 7-2 on pages 126 and 127. In it I show a family projecting an increase in net worth from $37,970 to $246,344 and a net income boost from $22,070 to $101,340 by year five.

"How can this be possible?" You may demand. "No one can expand their net worth by that much let alone more than triple their income in five years!" You are mistaken. Many people have achieved this and more even faster through intelligent investing and money management. To accomplish this you must do three things:

1. First believe it is possible.
2. Commit to the possibility in writing.
3. Open your mind to the ways you may achieve your goal.

"But your example shows salary income tripling. I can't make that kind of money on my present job," you say. That may be true. You may have to find new work, go back to school, start a business, take a second job, put a spouse to work, whatever. Committing to a five-year earnings figure that now seems beyond reach will inspire your wealth-building thoughts. I like to set a goal that triples my present earnings, because even if I reach only half of my targeted increase I'll still be 100% ahead of where I now am!

WHERE TO START?

Using the form I gave in Chapter Six (see Figure 6-13), determine your net worth for the current year. Then use the figures to help you project your net worth assets for next year on the format provided in Figure 7-1. This includes everything except cash. Cash will be affected by your savings goal. Pencil in what you believe you'll have in cash[1] by the end of the current year.

Next turn to the income portion of the form. Project your income and make a savings goal. Determine how your savings will be apportioned among your assets. For most of you, in the first and second years, your savings will go to cash accounts, so add this amount to the cash figure you've already penciled-in. Also add the amount of interest you expect to earn.

Now move over to the fifth year of the form and enter the net worth figure you'd like to achieve. Remember, your net worth is your level of wealth so make the sum large enough to be inspirational but not so large it is implausible. As you work through the plan you'll be able to determine the yearly steps needed to achieve your fifth year goal. For now just enter a figure.

Next move on to your projected earnings for year five of your plan. Take your current total income and triple it. Enter that amount. If you just can't accept tripling your income, then double it. If you only achieve half your earnings goal you'll be 50% ahead of your present income.

But salary alone will not make you wealthy. The next part is where imagination and planning come together. Your net worth growth is linked directly to your earnings and savings power. Therefore you must look for other sources of income. These include investment income in the form of interest, dividends,

---

[1] *Cash = savings and money market accounts.*

Figure 7-2: The Next-Five Planner*

(Plan Period: 19_91_ to 19_95_)

	19 _91_	19 _92_	19 _93_	19 _94_	19 _95_
I. Income Assets					
A. Net Earnings (1+2+3)	22,000.	36,000.	61,000.	69,000.	85,000.
(1) Primary job	22,000.	28,000.	44,500 NEW JOB	47,000.	53,500.
(2) Part-time (Mrs.)	—	8,000.	9,000.	14,000 MRS. F.T.	18,000.
(3) Free Lance (Mr.)	—	—	7,500.	8,000.	13,500.
B. Interest/Dividends	70.00	530.	11,170.	1,586.	3,500.
C. Rent/Business Inc	—	—	10,800. 2 APTS RENT=$450EA.	3,500 = STOCKS GAIN 11,500. RENT	12,840. RENT
Total Income (A–C)	22,070.	36,530.	82,970.	85,586.	101,340.
II. Other Assets		BUY 100 SHARES		SELL 100 BUY 300 SHARES	
A. Securities	—	2,800.	3,080.	12,500.	13,625.
B. IRAs/Vested Pensions	3,900.	1,650.	13,780.	24,364.	43,454.
C. Real Estate	55,000. CONDO	57,000.	155,000.	161,400.	180,900.
D. Autos/Boats/Planes	8,000.	6,500.	4,200.	2,800.	21,500. BUY CAR
E. Gold/Jewelry	1,100.	1,150.	1,200.	1,200.	1,250
F. Valuables/Collections	—	—	—	—	2,250. DIAMOND WATCH
G. Insurance-Cash Value	650.	725.	885.	950.	1,175.
H. Redeemable Deposits	—	—	—	—	—
I. Furniture/Miscellaneous	800.	800.	1,000.	1,000.	1,200.
Total Other Assets (A–I)	69,450.	76,575.	179,145	210,214	265,354

*For illustration purposes only.

Figure 7-2: The Next-Five Planner, *Cont'd*

(*Plan Period: 19 91 to 19 95*)

	19 91	19 92	19 93	19 94	19 95
III. Cash					
A. Checking Accounts	500.	500.	500.	500.	500.
B. Money Markets/CDs	4,000.	8,500.	5,500.	8,500.	21,500.
Total Cash	4,500.	9,000.	6,000.	9,000.	22,000.
IV. Liabilities					
A. Mortgage(s)	49,500.	48,775.	131,750.	130,850.	130,350.
B. Auto Loans	5,700.	2,499	-0-	-0-	12,000.
C. Credit Cards	2,300.	1,100.	-0-	-0-	-0-
D. Other	550. PROP. TAX	550. PROP. TAX	2,400. APT. EXP.	2,950. APT. EXP.	3,600. APT. EXP.
Total Liabilites					
V. NET WORTH (I+II+III–IV)	37,970.	69,181.	136,365.	173,950.	246,344.
SAVINGS GOAL (% of Net Income)	10%	20%	15%	20%	25%

Goals:

19 **91** INCREASE SAVINGS BY 2,000 — to $4,000.

19 **92** REDUCE CREDIT CARD BALANCE BY 50%., BUY 100 SHARES UTILITY STOCK (TOTAL = 2,800.), MRS. TO GET PART TIME JOB NETTING 8,000.

19 **93** PAYOFF CREDIT CARD DEBT & CAR LOAN, SELL CONDO, BUY 3-FLAT APT VALUED @ 155,000, GET NEW JOB NETTING $44,500 YR., START P.T. INSUR. SALES & EARN 7500 NET.

19 **94** MRS. GETS F.T. JOB & EARNS 14,000, SELL 100 SHARES BOUGHT IN 1992 @ 3,500. PROFIT. BUY 300 SHARES OF AN UNDERVALUED STOCK @ $12,500

19 **95** BUY NEW CAR FOR $21,500 AND DIAMOND WATCH FOR $2,250. INCREASE INSURANCE COMMISSIONS TO $13,500.

and capital gains. Another source may be free-lance or part-time business income. Yet another may be gains earned from the sale of collectibles, real estate, or antiques.

Start with the known. If you don't have any savings, make it your first-year goal to set up an account. Calculate how much you plan to save and how much interest it will earn, and add that to your net worth for the first year of your plan.

If you have a savings account, make it your goal to increase your total savings by X dollars. Also make it a goal to earn a higher rate of interest on your savings than you did in the past year. Add this total to your net worth for the first year.

Next turn to your salary for the second year of your plan and give yourself a healthy raise of, say, 15% to 25%. Most of us underestimate the earning power of our present job. We allow fate to determine what we'll be paid, hoping silently that some day we'll be discovered. Earlier I talked about dreaming, but this is not what I meant.

Take a proactive stance. Decide how you can increase your value as an employee so that you deserve the raise you're projecting. Ask your boss how you can earn it. Be creative! Think not only in terms of a promotion or raise but also how you may structure a yearly bonus or commission. But whatever you do, don't tell anybody that you want to increase your income so you can become wealthy or because you need it. Your needs are not important to employers. What they want to hear is how you can help them achieve their purpose.

What if you hit a brick wall? What if there is no chance for raises, bonuses, or promotions! Well, then it's time to rethink your career. It's time to look for new opportunities. This can be stated in your plan as your second- or third-year goal:

By 19_____ I'll secure a job earning $_____.

As you can see, when you set goals you obligate yourself to develop a plan of action to reach them. However, the farther you project in time, the less precisely you can plan how you'll get there. This is particularly true if you set high goals. This is perfectly all right. It allows you to use your creative imagination and play the What If game.

It works like this. "Three years from now, *what if* I take $40,000 of my savings and buy a handy man's special building in a prime suburban location? I know that many locations near my home have realized annual increases in property value of 4%. That means on a building valued at $200,000 I'll have a projected gain in net worth of $34,000 in year four and $43,330 in year five. But, if the building I buy is priced below market value by, say, $40,000, after I complete the repairs and sell the building, my total two-year gain could be $60,000 instead!"

CREATING MONEY CONSCIOUSNESS

I told you earlier how I smiled when I wrote down what I thought was an absurd net worth figure of $100,000 shortly after I returned to work. The figure seemed unreachable, but I wrote it down anyway in a type of child-like play. What I was doing was making an unconscious promise to achieve that figure. As it turned out, I realized that goal in three years instead of five through a fortunate combination of stock and real estate investments.

What you do when you write out a plan is help create money consciousness. This is reinforced by your recording of daily expenses and by running your home like a business. You become vigilant and watchful and so tuned-in to money-making opportunities that they seem to be magically attracted to you.

What is really happening is that you are seeing the entire picture as a sum of the parts. You are viewing the entire puzzle and seeing both the pictured scene and each individual piece simultaneously. That's the power of planning!

A final exercise I like to do is to establish one major financial goal for each of the five years. I state the goal on the bottom of my plan.

I look at my plan every month and revise it whenever I feel it's necessary. One thing that I failed to mention is the need for opportunity research. In the Gold Rush Days prospectors would find a likely looking piece of earth and start digging. It was pretty hit and miss. Your wealth-building activities needn't be so speculative.

There is an abundance of written sources to help you. I cite some specific references you can find at your local library later in this book and I have also provided a small bibliography. Make daily reading of financial papers and magazines a regular part of your life. Make the pursuit of wealth as routine as brushing your teeth. By doing this you will see the opportunities that others miss and be ready to sell when they finally wake up to buy. You'll be rewarded handsomely for your foresight.

A friend of mine claims the reason I have done so well in investing is because it's my hobby. I guess with all the time I devote to my pursuit it must look that way. Well the truth is that it's not my hobby. It's my profession. A hobby is done for the fun of it, with little or no thought to the profits that may be generated. Most of the time a hobby is a money-loser rather than a money-gainer.

I do what I do for one purpose: To become independent-ly wealthy so my family may live comfortably for the rest of our lives. This dream is available to everyone. But you have to quit just dreaming. Draw upon all your creative powers! Think, imagine, dream, ponder, research. But most important . . . *start planning today!*

CHAPTER **8**

What To Do with Your Savings: The Basics

When I first contemplated an investment program, a number of things confused me. One thing I wondered about was how to determine when a security is a good buy. Prices change daily. Some go down and never seem to go up again, and vice versa. Others bounce around so much it seems impossible to judge their true value. Finding a good investment at an excellent price seemed extraordinarily difficult, though I was determined to discover how.

A GOOD RETURN FOR A SAFE INVESTMENT

Another thing I puzzled about was what is a good rate of return for a safe investment. I knew that there had to be a better rate than passbook savings, but I was unsure how high a rate you could ask for before an investment becomes unduly risky. I didn't even realize that an investment producing lower interest, like a bond, could be risky at all.

Even more basic, I didn't know that there is a difference between an investment and a speculation. Nor did I realize that many investments are really gambles. Like most folks the only knowledge of investing I had were friends' stories about someone they knew who made it big in stocks and parlayed a relatively small amount of money into a great fortune. The stories were exciting but, curiously, the folks they knew never had a name. If they did, I certainly never met any of them.

Can you make it big in investments? The answer is an emphatic yes! How about making it big with a small stake? The answer is a tentative yes. It stands to reason that a small stake will require a larger return than a large stake to achieve the same result. For example, for $50,000 to double in value to $100,000 in 10 years would require an investment yielding 7.5% annually with all proceeds reinvested, whereas for $1,000 to increase to $100,000 in 10 years would require an investment yielding 53% annually.

What kind of investments yield 50% or higher? According to the definition I use for an investment . . . none! The only instruments that could possibly produce average annual returns at that level are so highly speculative they would be outright gambles!

Before I attempt to tell you what's a good return for a safe investment, let's take a broader perspective and ask: What's a good profit for most businesses in the United States? Before I started my investment program I had a very naive view of the kind of profits made by U.S. corporations. To me, they were all money-making machines that heartlessly extracted huge sums of money from consumers for profits of 50% or more. It was a shock to learn that the net after-tax profits of many U.S. corporations range from 3% to 5%, with a high of 7% or 8%. Major institutional investors like insurance companies and large pension funds are happy with annual returns of 7% to 8% or an inflation-adjusted rate of 2% to 3% above the Consumer Price Index.

What this means is that all the big guys are looking for profits amounting to pennies on each dollar! This is an important concept to remember. It prevents us from falling victim to unnecessarily risky investments or con jobs offered by investment criminals. It helps us keep our perspective.

Investment risk is determined by potential return. In general, the more an investment can return, the higher the risk. For example, junk bonds are so named because they have a great chance of failing. They also yield a high rate of interest. How high? Usually only four or five[1] percentage points more interest than high-quality, secure investments like U.S. Treasury Notes. So why would anyone invest in them? That's a million-dollar question that can only be answered by saying, it depends on each investor's individual situation. For small investors it's safe to say that junk bonds are not an investment option.

The Three Little Pigs

Investment risk can be compared to the childhood story of the "Three Little Pigs." The first pig's house of straw can be compared to gambles. They take little thought, require little money, are easy to put together—and are extremely vulnerable to failure when any ill economic wind blows. The second pig's house of sticks are speculations. These are somewhat more difficult to construct but involve relatively little cost. They can produce large gains but also have a greater chance of failure than success. The third pig's house of bricks is a conservative investment program. Built slowly over time and fortified with large cash holdings, these programs offer investors regular income and potential for large gains over time with limited risk.

I said earlier that a small-stake high-flier didn't comply with my definition of an investment. How then do I define an investment? I prefer to use the definition offered by a man whose book I mention in the recommended readings. His name is Benjamin Graham, and he is distinguished by having made

---

[1] *In investment lingo four to five hundred basis points.*

money in the stock market during The Great Depression of the 1930s. That alone was quite an accomplishment!

How did this investment wizard define an investment? Although he has several qualifications for what constitutes a *good* investment, he was explicit in his definition of an investment itself. To him, *an investment is a financial instrument that conserves capital and offers growth and income.* Growth is the appreciation of capital (the money you invested). Income is dividends and interest.

You'll note that the first criterion for an investment is the preservation of capital. Graham stressed the importance of preserving capital throughout all his books. He reasoned that potential for huge gains is unimportant if you are at high risk of losing capital. In his thinking, a program of large gains and losses is inferior to a program of moderate gains with no losses. Therefore, cardinal to his theories is preservation of capital.

The next most important thing is that an investment should have an opportunity for capital appreciation or growth. How much growth potential is a function of cost. That is, the cheaper you can buy the asset the greater its growth potential. Finally, an investment should produce an assurance of income. By Graham's definition a stock without a dividend cannot be an investment because it gives no guarantee of income. By his definition, investments would be: Stocks with dividends, corporate and government bonds and notes, and selected mutual funds.

By contrast, a speculation is an opportunity that risks capital against possible future gains. Speculations, usually offer no income assurances; if they do produce income, they offer high yields—and high risk. Examples of speculations include non-income-producing real estate, low-rated or junk bonds, and stocks with a high price-earnings ratio[1] that don't pay a dividend.

---

[1] *A stock's P.E. is listed beside its price on the financial pages. Graham would consider a stock with a P.E. greater than 12 to be speculative.*

Gambles expose your capital to total loss. Gains can be great and are highly leveraged: You can use a small amount of capital to control a large financial position with the goal of magnifying the potential gain. For example, a stock option allows you to benefit from a stock gain or loss for a fraction of the cost of owning the stocks itself. On a percentage basis, your gain can be sizeable—50% or higher.

However, options are limited to a specific period of time: 45, 60, 90, or 120 days. If you haven't sold your option for a profit by the time it expires, you lose your entire investment. Stock options are examples of what is referred to as wasting assets. Examples of other gambles include futures contracts, oil and gas exploration contracts, and penny stocks.

I've given you much more information than you'll need at this stage of your wealth-building program. Do not contemplate an investment program in securities until you've constructed a solid cash foundation. The goal of this book is to help you develop that foundation. We will therefore confine the scope of investments to cash instruments. I recommend, however, that you begin as soon as possible familiarizing yourself with the entire field of investments.

I have touched on a few of the more advanced concepts only to make you aware of them Resist the temptation to plunge into an investment you don't understand, no matter how good it sounds or who advises you. There are no safe shortcuts.

I know firsthand how difficult it is to be patient with so many marvelous-sounding claims floating about Even as an experienced investor, I've lost money a few times by disobeying my own investment rules. Protect your capital. Be patient. Your wealth will accumulate faster than you think—but never as fast as you want. For your own protection I suggest you consider adopting my number one sacred rule of investing: Never invest in anything you do not personally thoroughly understand!

CASH INSTRUMENTS

A prudent investment program begins with a strong cash base. There are a variety of instruments for holding cash and earning income. We will deal with the basics, excluding passbook savings accounts, which I consider adequate only for small cash holdings of one or two hundred dollars.

Money market accounts—available from banks, savings and loans, mutual fund companies, and brokerage houses—are excellent cash instruments. All have a *dollar-per-share par value.* This means that the dollar value of your account will remain stable. It will not fluctuate with changing market conditions.

Generally speaking, the lowest rates of interest are offered by banking institutions and the highest by mutual fund companies. Interest rates cluster about the prime rate and usually are two to three percentage points above the inflation rate. They are backed by a variety of *money instruments* including commercial paper, retail repurchase agreements, certificates of deposit, U.S. and foreign government securities, time deposits, and even tax-free municipal bonds.

Money market accounts which are totally supported by U.S. government securities are considered the safest but yield about a half percentage point less interest than regular accounts. You can even get an account free from federal income tax, but these accounts pay significantly less interest. Whether or not a tax-free account is better for you depends on your tax bracket and the interest rate offered.

Almost all money market accounts offer free check-writing privileges. With bank and savings and loan accounts there may be some restriction as to the number of checks you may write per month. With brokerage and mutual fund accounts you are usually restricted to writing checks of $500 or more.

If you don't have a money market account you should investigate opening one as soon as possible, especially if you are holding $500 or more in a passbook savings account. The reason is that your passbook account consistently produces a low rate of interest, usually around 5 1/2%, regardless of the current rate of inflation. This means you actually lose money during periods of high inflation and rising interest rates.

Certificates of Deposit are another bank option. CD interest rates tend to be one-half to a percentage point higher than money market accounts, but not always. Most have significant penalties for early withdrawals, but a new version now on the market carries no penalties. Brokers offer high interest CDs from out-of-state banks that carry interest rates that are several points higher than local rates. Usually these CDs are from banks and savings and loans that are having financial difficulties. Although they are insured by federal deposit insurance they still make me nervous.

One thing to keep in mind with CDs is the term of commitment they require. Stay as short-term as possible. Interest rates today can fluctuate up or down as much as a percentage point and a half in a single year. To take advantage of interest rate movements in either direction, try to buy CDs with terms of less than one year and that will also allow renewal at the same rate of interest. Last, there's considerable competition in this market so search hard for the best interest rates, terms, and conditions.

MORE SOPHISTICATED INVESTMENTS

How much money should you have before you consider more sophisticated investments? Enough to lose! That's possibly harsh, but it is true. Once you move away from cash instruments into mutual funds, stocks, and bonds, you no longer have a stable dollar-per-share par value. This means that the value of the cash you invest may go up or down depending on market conditions at the time of withdrawal. For example, the $10,000 you invest in a mutual fund in September may only be worth

$9,850 in October, $9,765 in November, $10,775 in December and $8,950 in January. If you need the entire $10,000 in January you're in trouble.

Those folks who are most likely to get in trouble in investing are those who are undercapitalized. They risk funds they can ill afford to lose. When markets turn unfavorable they ride their loss, hoping for a turnaround, because they can't afford the loss of even one dollar. When the turnaround doesn't come they panic and sell for an even greater loss. If they had sufficient capital they probably could have waited out the crisis and quite likely earned a profit to boot.

Therefore, I believe you should have at least $10,000 in cash before you consider investing in a mutual fund and you should commit no more than half your cash to the investment. For stocks, I feel that you should have at least $25,000 in cash and commit no more than $15,000 to stocks. I have three reasons why I believe you need more cash for investments in stocks than in mutual funds:

1. $15,000 allows you to buy round lots of 100 shares instead of odd lots of less than 100, which are harder and more costly to sell.
2. This amount of money lets you buy shares from at least two different companies. This helps to spread your risk slightly.
3. Having $10,000 in cash left after your stock investment enables you to take a long-term perspective of six months to a year or more, and avoid costly and ineffective frequent stock buying and selling.

The Biggest Investment You'll Ever Make

Those were the words of the realtor who sold me my first house nearly 20 years ago. At the time it was a sizable investment of cash for me, but it also produced a gain three times the size of my cash down payment three years later when I sold the home.

Over the past 40 years we Americans have become so used to making money on residential real estate that it came as a major shock when property values in certain areas started falling in the late 1980s. In truth, falling real estate values had been predicted by investment experts for years, but it was difficult to accept such predictions during periods of sharp price increases. The problem with residential real estate is basically one of perception.

Is residential real estate still a good investment? A better question is, Was it ever? By the Graham definition I gave you, residential real estate was never an investment to start with. It was and is a speculation whose value is wholly dependent on future market conditions and actions. An investment, as we have defined, must have an assurance of income. Residential real estate has no income whatsoever.

Does that mean we shouldn't buy homes, condos, townhouses, or co-ops? Not at all! What it means is that we must change our viewpoint on home ownership and enter all transactions aware of what they mean today. We must be more careful than ever before about where, what, how, and when we buy. But most important we must view homes for what they truly are . . . places to live.

The exception to this is commercial real estate and rental property. These are and will remain investments. However, you must use extreme caution when purchasing them to assure that the property will continue to be profitable. There are entire books written on the topic, so we will stop here.

Rent or Buy, Which is Better?

There's both a quantitative and qualitative answer to this question. It's relatively easy to determine whether or not a home is a good financial decision for you. One way is to use last year's income tax form. Fill out the itemized deductions as if you owned the home already. If you enjoy a tax refund, subtract the refund from your total payments for the year and divide that figure by 12. Compare it with your rent payment. Most likely your rent will be less. The difference will be even greater if you add to your monthly payment the other costs that are unique to home ownership like maintenance and heating costs. Now look at the resulting payment. Can you comfortably afford it? Yes or no? There are, of course, qualitative factors that can't be computed that you may also need to consider. For example, a home may be a better environment for raising children, it's more private, etc.

Some caveats! Tax deductions are not sacred. As Congress giveth, it can also taketh away. In fact, there have been rumblings about elimination of the homeowners' deduction for years, though it has never come about. That doesn't mean the deduction is secure. The latest Congressional thought is to limit rather than eliminate the deduction. With Congress in the mood for taking away privileges, I expect we'll see something in the form of a deduction ceiling in the not-too-distant future.

Negotiating Real Estate Deals

Realtors say there are three key factors in determining a property's value: Location, Location, Location. So after you find the right location, the next thing to do is find a real opportunity. Since home purchases are such an emotional experience, the more cold logic you can bring to the bargaining table the better the advantage you'll have. Find a house that is well-built and structurally sound but a bit on the shabby side. You know . . . a house whose owners haven't taken proper care of the lawn and landscaping, have allowed paint to discolor and peel, haven't decorated since the Fifties, or just have terrible taste.

The first house my wife and I bought was such a house. When I first showed it to her she told me she wouldn't live in it because it was too ugly. Ugly, yes, but it was structurally sound, and in a prime suburban neighborhood, and it had many hidden but interesting architectural features. Two years of hard work and a little cash enabled us to sell the same house 26 months later for nearly twice the price we paid for it.

Empty Houses = Potentially Good Deals

An empty house[1] is a good sign. It means that the owners could not wait to sell it before moving and therefore should be highly motivated to sell. But whether empty or occupied, look for houses with the oldest listing dates. Generally speaking the longer a house is on the market the more anxious the buyers are to sell. This is particularly true if a job transfer is pending where the company will not purchase the house, an estate settlement is pending, or the owners have already bought another home. Have your broker try to get as much information as possible about the reasons for the sale to help you determine the seller's level of desperation.

Search the house for defects that can be used to justify your offer. Look for outdated kitchen and bathroom fixtures, cracked sidewalks, worn carpeting, walls in need of painting or papering, roof problems, appliances (furnace, water heater, stoves) that will need to be replaced. Assemble a price list of similar-sized houses in the area and make your first offer at least 10% to 20% below the lowest-priced. Personally I like to start a bit lower . . . 20% to 30%. Make your price conditional

---

[1] *The empty houses I'm referring to are previously owned and occupied homes, not new ones. However, new houses that have sat empty for six months or more can also be great buys!*

upon repair or improvement of several items like repaired sidewalks or a new kitchen sink.

Be prepared to have your offer rejected. When it is, delete a repair or two and resubmit your offer. But don't touch the price. Let it ride until the third offer. Continue submitting until you get the price and conditions you want.

You'll probably get an argument from your realtor with these kind of tactics. His argument will probably run along the lines that you should offer a "fair price." I look at real estate from a three-price perspective: best price, fair price, and *my price*! If you shop long enough, you'll be able to determine what a bargain price should be. Make sure you get it!

Most states require that all offers, no matter how absurd, be presented to the sellers. However, an uncooperative realtor can put a chill on your offer. If you get a great deal of resistance, find another realtor to present your offer. Remember, unless you're paying the realtor a fee to find you a house, he represents the seller only. Since realtors are paid on commission, it is in their best interest to get you to pay the highest possible price!

Creativity, P-l-e-a-s-e

Sometimes a little imagination can net you big bonuses in difficult negotiations. Think about how you can creatively structure a real estate deal so it's to your best advantage. A friend of mine used this kind of strategy to buy the house of his dreams for a bargain price.

The house he wanted was the object of a divorce settlement. The settlement allowed the ex-wife to live in the house for as long as it took to sell the house, with the husband responsible for all payments. Upon the sale the proceeds would be shared equally by both partners.

The house seemed to be exactly what my friend was looking for. The location was right, and so were the structure and the price. But, when he was shown the house it was a mess. Dishes in the sink, unclean bathrooms, wallpaper hanging from the walls that looked as if it had been purposely peeled, lawn uncut. It appeared to him that the house was being purposely trashed by the wife to sabotage any potential sale.

He reasoned that any offer, no matter how reasonable, would be automatically rejected by the wife. The husband, on the other hand, was highly motivated, since he would have to continue making payments until a sale was transacted. An idea struck him. He would offer to buy the husband's share of the house and inform the wife that his family would be happy to share the house with her if she didn't want to sell. He checked with his lawyer to see if it was legal to buy a partner's share of a jointly owned home. He was told it was.

He instructed his realtor to present a two-part offer to the husband. The first part was for purchase of the entire home. The second part was for purchase of only his share if his ex-wife rejected the offer. The husband agreed to and signed both offers. When the wife was presented with the first offer, she was informed that if she rejected it, her husband had already agreed to sell his share to my friend. The realtor also told her that my friend felt that the house was big enough for her and his family to share.

She agreed to sell the house.

HOW AM I DOING?

Everyone needs a benchmark to determine how well he is doing with his investments. I like to use The Consumer Price Index, published by the U.S. Department of Commerce. The CPI is the rate of inflation for the year. If your return was greater than the

CPI, you made money. If it was less, you lost money. It's as simple as that.

I mentioned doing investment research several times in this book. The place to start is your public library. Most libraries have enormous financial resources including subscriptions to references used by brokerage houses like *Value Line Reports, Standard & Poor's,* and *O.T.C. Reports* as well as a host of financial books, magazines, and newspapers. Get acquainted with the treasures in your local library.

Should you want to start building your own personal investment library as well, the publisher of this book, *International Publishing*, has an excellent collection of sophisticated titles. You may write for a catalog at the address in the front of this book.

A final word on investing: Is there ever a place for speculation and a gamble? As long as there are people on Earth there will be speculations and gambles, and you could be lucky enough to profit by them. If you must gamble or speculate do so as Ben Graham advised, with your eyes wide open. Realize that you're gambling and commit no more than 10% of your portfolio to it.

I've taken this advice and limited my speculations to 5% of my portfolio. I must report, however, that in every case I lost money! Speculations and gambles make promises. Investments pay off.

CHAPTER 9

The Reality of Taxes

No good wealth-building plan would be complete without taking into account an area that can gobble up a third or more of a person's gross income. That area is taxes. How much you pay in taxes depends to a certain degree on your knowledge of the available opportunities. While I believe that you should take advantage of every possible benefit available, I don't believe that anyone should go to extremes to avoid taxes. Reason? Like all financial matters, extremes are laden with risk. Taxes can be a dual-edged sword. On the one hand are investment criminals eager to prey upon the naive and uninformed by offering "tax shelters"; and on the other hand is the IRS, constantly monitoring returns for errors and fraud. A bad investment decision, poor judgment, or both can result in loss of capital, heavy penalties and fines, or worse!

The reality is that it's your responsibility as an American citizen to pay your fair share of taxes. But that doesn't mean overpaying! This chapter addresses *decisions you must make to reduce your tax bill* and *actions you may take to keep it from growing any bigger.*

THE MOOD OF CONGRESS

The 1986 Tax Act significantly changed the way we figure our taxes. The change brought about some of the lowest tax rates in history and eliminated loopholes that were costly to the economy. However, it also reduced or eliminated many deductions and adjustments we were accustomed to using, including the deductions for consumer debt interest and local sales taxes, business expense deductions, income averaging, IRA deductions, and various trust schemes created to reduce taxes by shifting income to children or by offsetting salary income with passive losses.

The result is a streamlined tax code that is healthier for all of us. The problem is keeping it that way.

The legislative and executive branches of the federal government are committed to reducing the federal deficit by $500 million by 1995. Polls indicate, however, that Congress does not have the backing of the American citizenry for plans to reduce the debt through broad-sweeping income tax hikes. To propose such increases would be political suicide.

So Congress and elected officials at all levels of government have cleverly avoided public confrontation by raising rates through selective taxation. These tactics have brought about an array of both apparent and hidden taxes ranging from excise taxes to luxury taxes and increases in user fees and permits. Because they target only select markets, be they beer drinkers or drivers of luxury cars, these tax increases are much easier to impose. It's another version of the politician's favorite old game of "stick it to the other guy." However, these new tax tactics are dangerous in that they may be harmful to business, inflationary, and precedents for even more costly indirect forms of taxation.

Some forms are darn right sneaky. Take a new series of taxes on the profits of foreign-based operations of multinational corporations. The purported goal of these transfer pricing taxes and penalties is to get foreign firms (Japanese in particular) to pay their fair share of U.S. taxes and by doing so to make American firms better able to compete. However, according to *Forbes*, these new taxes could hurt American companies more than they help them:

U.S. multi-internationals are the big targets. Consider in the new tax plan the 20% to 40% penalties designed to punish underpayments by multi-internationals. The penalties apply to U.S. and foreign firms alike. Moreover, any assault on foreign firms will simply squeeze American firms even harder as foreign tax authorities retaliate against U.S. multi-internationals operating within their borders (*Forbes*, November 26, 1990, p. 171).

Undoubtedly these new taxes will further handicap American competitiveness in the world market and result in lower profits for U.S. companies, fewer opportunities stateside for American citizens, and higher prices for products. Brilliant!

The luxury tax is another sneaky tax that may be a trial-balloon for a much broader-based European-style value added tax (VAT). Like luxury taxes, VATs are levied as a percentage of the value of the product. In Europe VATs are in the vicinity of 15% to 18% and are applied to virtually every product from food and shoes to business equipment. VATs have a negative effect on consumption, because when prices rise without wages being raised, consumers react by buying less.

VATs are hazardous for a second reason: When products are taxed at the manufacturer level, the tax disappears into the price of the product. Since all the consumer sees is a price increase, he blames the increase on the manufacturer, instead of on government, where it belongs. Even if the tax is shown on a price tag or invoice, there's still a risk that consumers will psychologically feel cheated by the company for passing along what they regard as the manufacturer's cost of doing business. Government, on the other hand, can go merrily along, increasing taxes at will with little public resistance.

The current luxury tax also has the potential to hurt the American economy directly. How? If you analyze which makes of cars will be most detrimentally affected by the tax, you'll discover that the brunt of tax will be borne by the purchasers of imported luxury makes. U.S. models are largely unaffected. The tax appears to be rather protectionistic.

On the surface this may seem positive. However, the long-term impact of protectionism is always detrimental, because with competition removed or limited, protected industries have little motivation to change. Remaining the same, they grow weaker and in need of more protective measures.

The U.S. steel industry is a good example. For many years the U.S. steel industry reigned supreme. After World War II the U.S. had most of the world market. Slowly Europe and most notably Japan started to catch up. During the Sixties and Seventies Japan and European manufacturers became net exporters of steel and began displacing the U.S. in world markets. However, the bulk of the steel U.S. companies produced went into automobiles, ships, and heavy equipment. The majority of these products were produced and sold in the U.S. leaving U.S. steel producer's primary markets relatively untouched.

However, when foreign steel producers also tried to enter the U.S. market, manufacturers cried foul and were able to establish protectionist barriers. Having a protected market gave them little incentive to modernize to stay competitive. Prices escalated with labor pressures and product demand until the bubble burst in the Seventies. Primary customers like automobile manufacturers cut orders due to lost market shares and substituted cheaper, more adaptable materials like plastics for steel. The entire U.S. ship building industry was lost to foreign builders who could build better ships overseas due to cheaper foreign steel and labor.

U.S. producers' of coke-fired furnaces also came under attack for air pollution. Air quality and environmental measures further added to their costs. Due to competitive pressures many of their primary manufacturing customers moved some or all of their manufacturing operations off-shore to take advantage of lower cost raw materials and cheaper labor.

Today the U.S. steel industry is a shadow of its former self. With outdated facilities and equipment, the steel industry can now barely compete in the U.S. let alone the world market. Many plants are closed. Operations nationwide are less than a third of what they were during their heyday. To a large degree the steel industry is a victim of its own security blanket—a protected market.

U.S. history is filled with such examples. This could have tragic implications for the U.S. automotive industry, which has finally begun to offer products that compete effectively with foreign models. A return to the old business-as-usual attitudes by U.S. carmakers could cost both the automotive industry and the U.S. economy dearly in the future.

A second industry which is largely dominated by U.S. manufacturers could be devastated by this tax. That is the recreational boating industry. For manufacturers of boats over 30 feet, nearly every model will be taxed. While boats may be a luxury for their owners, they represent employment for thousands of skilled and semi-skilled workers throughout the United States. A slowdown in boat purchases will mean lost jobs. In fact, Representative Bob Davis (R-Mich) is reported as saying, in a January 24, 1991 *Chicago Tribune* article by John Husar, that one marine trade association is already predicting up to 8,000 people may lose their jobs as a result of the boating industry slump. In the same report, Jeff Napier, president of the National Marine Manufacturers Association, said the irony "of the whole thing is that it was a big symbolic gesture to tax the rich. What it did was put a whole lot of blue-collar people out of work. . . . It's dumb economics and dumb politics." Amen!

Another sneaky tax, or rather a tax increase, is the reduction of personal exemptions and deductions for high-income taxpayers. At first glance a typical reaction may be, "If someone makes $100 grand or $150 grand, they should pay more taxes. Who cares if they lose their exemptions and deductions?" This is precisely the kind of reaction Congress wants. It divides us and plays into the "stick it to the other guy" political ploy. Worse yet, it sets a precedent and government loves this kind of precedent, because it builds the case for expansion of the program: Once you limit deductions and exemptions for one income group, there's nothing to stop Congress from lowering the ceiling next year, again the following year, over and over until nearly everyone is affected. What a wonderful way to raise taxes . . . all without raising rates! In 1991, the top tax rate will be lowered from 33% to 31%, but, despite the reduction, taxes will actually increase due to the termination of tax breaks. Now that's what I call sneaky!

As taxes are raised special interests will demand exception and sheltering, from which usually only the strongest and richest interests benefit. Over time the code will once again become littered with exceptions, isolated and protected by carefully-worded tax terminology. A quick look at the complications involved in determining passive versus active income and losses proves the point. The more complicated tax law becomes, the more difficult it is for the average citizen to understand. In the end the average taxpayer picks up the tab.

WHAT YOU CAN DO TO REDUCE YOUR TAXES

The changes for 1990-91 can be characterized as more of the same, just a little worse. All deductions and adjustments have remained, with an expansion of a few and liberalization of some others. But be careful about the use of the business deductions, those for home offices in particular. Returns filed with these deductions will be carefully scrutinized and may trigger audits.

This chapter will give you a general overview of what you can do to limit or reduce your federal income tax. It is not intended to be a primary source for tax planning. Since taxes depend on individual circumstances, I advise you to seek the advice of a tax accountant, lawyer, or other tax professional.

Before we begin, I wish to cover something that bothered me needlessly for years. Every year near tax time the same old anxiety came over me. When the form finally arrived my anxiety approached hysteria . . . even when all I was required to file was the short form. Only by shuffling off to some tax service would I enjoy relief. One year when I was short on cash, I decided to try doing my own taxes using the previous year's form as a model. I discovered that preparation was not as intimidating as I had imagined. Truth was, if I used a calculator and followed the form step by step, tax preparation was rather easy. I was thrilled! In the years that followed, I tried more complicated forms and began reading tax guides as a regular part of my financial discipline.

I urge you to do the same. To be a financial success, you must not allow anything to intimidate you. You must be comfortable with figures, calculating, and legal and financial language. For most of us these things don't come easily, but with continued practice they can be conquered.

Realize that we're limited by beliefs that have been formed by prior negative learning experiences. Over time these beliefs convince us that there are certain things we can't do. The best way to overcome this is by retraining, that is, by doing the things we're certain we can't do.

Does this mean we shouldn't ever use tax professionals? No! I use a CPA. But by arming myself with substantial knowledge of current tax laws, I can get more value from his help.

Figure 9-1 gives the tax rates for 1990 and 1991. There will be no change in 1990 rates. However, in 1991 top tax rates of 28% and 33% will be merged into a new single rate of 31%.

What appears to be a break for the top-rate taxpayers is an illusion. The lowering of the rate is more than balanced by the loss of deductions and personal exemptions.

Your primary deductions will arise from home ownership. It's one of the few remaining deductions that is universally

Figure 9-1: Tax Rates: 1990–1991

Tax Income Brackets—1990

		Annual Taxable Income		
Tax Rate	Married Filing Joint	Head of Household	Single	Married Filing Seperately
15%	0-32,450	0-26,050	0-19,450	0-16,225
28%	32,451-78,400	26,051-67,200	19,451-47,050	16,226-39,200
33%	78,401-162,770	67,201-134,930	47,051-97,620	39,201-123,570
28%	Over 162,770	Over 134,930	Over 97,620	Over 123,570

Tax Income Brackets—1991

15%	0-32,450	0-26,050	0-19450	0-16,225
28%	32,451-78,400	26,051-67,200	19,451-47,050	16,226-39,200
31%	Over 78,400	Over 67,200	Over 47,050	Over 39,200

available to all taxpayers. For taxpayers earning less than $100,000, primary residence deductions are entirely deductible. Taxpayers earning more than $100,000, however, are subject to special phase-in limitations.

As in years past, mortgage interest and local property taxes for a personal residence are completely deductible. However, upon sale of your home the proceeds of the sale may be taxable as ordinary income if a gain[1] is realized. However, if the proceeds are invested in another principal residence within two years, taxes may be deferred, provided the new home's purchase price is equal to the adjusted sale price of the former residence. Sales expenses and fixing-up expenses may be deducted from the gross sale price to determine the adjusted sales price. Any future taxable gain will be based on this adjusted sales price.

---

[1] *A gain results when a property sells for a price greater than what was originally paid plus improvements.*

A once-in-a-lifetime tax exclusion is available to taxpayers over 55 years of age for up to $125,000 of any gain realized from the sale of a principal residence. However, the property must have been used by the taxpayer as his or her principal residence for the last three out of five years preceding the date of the sale.

The 1986 Tax Act also clarified the definition of what qualifies as a vacation residence. A vacation home may now include certain boats and recreational vehicles as well as a cottage, a house, or a condominium. Mortgage interest and local property taxes are fully deductible, but there must be personal use of the property to qualify. Personal use means that the taxpayer has used the property in the preceding year for 14 days or 10% of the number of days the property is rented at fair market value, whichever is greater.

If the property is rented for less than ten days, the gross income is excluded from taxes and no deductions other than interest and taxes are allowed. If rented for more than 15 days, the deductions are allocated between the rental and personal use. Deductions attributed to the rental use may not exceed the rental income earned. Excess deductions may be carried forward and applied against future rental income. Special vacation rules apply. Check with your local IRS office or tax professional for further details.

The tax act also clarified the rules for the deductibility of mortgage points. Under the current law, all points paid to secure a loan for the purchase or improvement of the principal residence are fully deductible. However, if you want the deduction, you have to write a separate check, not have the points deducted from the loan proceeds. Points associated with refinancing are amortized over the term of the loan.

Other costs in obtaining a home such as transfer fees, title and survey fees, lawyer fees, and sales commissions are added to the home's original purchase price thus reducing the amount of any future capital gain that is subject to taxation.

Rental Property Deductions—Watch Out

Abuses during the late Seventies and early Eighties of real estate investment schemes devised to reduce taxes on earned income via investments losses prompted lawmakers to devise stringent rules for investment property deductions. According to the code, real estate investments must be identified as active, passive, or portfolio. *Rental real estate is automatically considered a passive activity regardless of the involvement of the taxpayer in the management of the property.* Generally speaking, passive losses may be only used to offset other sources of passive income. However, some taxpayers with adjusted gross incomes of $100,000 or less who actively participate in the management of the property may qualify for an exception that will let them offset up to $25,000 of net income from other categories including wages. This deduction is phased out over incomes between $100,000 and $150,000. Once again, check with your local IRS Office or see your tax professional for particulars.

Consumer Debt Deduction . . . Going, Going, Gone

The deduction for consumer debt will be totally phased out after 1990. However, you may still deduct existing consumer debt interest and automotive loans obtained via refinancing through a home equity loan. Home equity loan interest payments are deductible up to the cost of the home plus improvements and limited to $100,000 of home equity.

Be careful: For many Americans the equity in their homes represents their primary investment. Borrowing against the equity reduces that investment and diminishes its potential as a financial safety cushion. In these days of uncertainty in the real estate market, borrowing against your equity may be risky. Should property values fall in your area and the equity in your property be borrowed up to its previous full value, you could end up with negative net worth. If you are forced to sell, you may have balances remaining due on your mortgage and equity loan—with no money left over. Many families in Texas faced this kind of economic situation in the early Eighties when the oil boom ended.

Educational Expenses—New Slant on an Old Problem

All educational expenses that add up to more than 2% of your adjusted gross income are deductible if they are for the purpose of improving or maintaining skills. You may not, however, deduct educational expenses involved in preparing for a new career or for your first real job.

Deductible expenses include tuition, books, fees, equipment, travel to and from the educational institution, and living expenses. Educational expenses for meeting general education prerequisites may be disallowed. Employer-paid educational expenses remain non-taxable and have been expanded to include graduate school.

As straightforward as the law is for adults, it is complicated for children. Again as a reaction to abuses in the former tax code, legislators created what is referred to as the Kiddie Tax. Simply stated, any unearned income of a minor child that exceeds $1,000 is taxed at the parent's rate.

The tax works like this. For all children under the age 14, the first $500 of their unearned income is tax-free. The next $500 is taxed at the child's 15% tax rate. Any excess is taxed at the parent's tax rate. The source of the assets is not considered. Thus even if the grandparents give the child the money, the investment income generated by it is subject to the tax. Once the child reaches age 14, he is treated as a separate taxpayer and no longer subject to these rules.

With the average cost of a four-year college education at a state university in the vicinity of $50,000, almost all taxpayers will have to deal with the Kiddie Tax at one time or another. Fortunately, Congress provided two tax exclusions for bona fide college savers. The first is for a Minor Trust. Up to $5,450 of income earned by the trust for the benefit of the minor is taxed at the 15% rate, but the trust must distribute all the accumulated income to the child before the child is 21. Any income distributed after that is subject to additional taxes.

A second exclusion is for the purchase of U.S. Savings Bonds (Series EE bonds). Bonds purchased for a child that matures after he reaches age 14 will shift to the child's normal tax bracket and will not be subject to the Kiddie Tax.

Series EE bonds issued after 1989 may also be used to fund higher education costs for adults. In this case, interest is excluded from taxable income if the bonds have been purchased after the taxpayer is 24. Funds may be used for higher education expenses for the taxpayer, spouse, or a dependent. The exclusion is phased out for married couples as their adjusted gross income increases from $60,000 to $90,000 and for singles from $40,000 to $55,000.

A better way to generate tax-free savings for educational expenses is to buy municipal bonds (discussed in the next section).

PAY TAXES WHEN YOUR INCOME IS LOWER

Under the current law, one of the best ways to reduce your taxes is to defer income until retirement. In this way it may be subject to lower taxes, because your income will be lower. The Individual Retirement Account or IRA is the primary vehicle for doing this.

The deduction remains unchanged: A working taxpayer may deduct up to $2,000 provided he or his spouse is not covered by a company-sponsored plan. If either spouse is covered by a company plan, the full deduction is available only to taxpayers whose adjusted gross income does not exceed

$40,000. The deduction is reduced proportionately for taxpayers whose gross incomes are between $40,000 and $50,000.

Single taxpayers who are covered by a company plan may also take the full $2,000 IRA deduction if their income does not exceed $25,000, and the deduction is proportionately reduced as income increases from $25,000 to $35,000.

An additional deduction of $250 is allowed for spousal IRAs when the spouse earns little income from employment. The deduction phase-out rules apply to spousal IRAs as well.

A non-deductible IRA contribution of up to $2,000 ($2,250 for spousal IRAs) is allowed for all others who do not qualify for deductible IRAs. A non-deductible IRA offers the tax-deferred benefits of a regular IRA.

If you do not have an IRA, start one this year. A wide variety of investments qualify, ranging from stocks to money market accounts. If you are qualified, it is one of your primary tax reduction opportunities. Take advantage of it.

Another way to defer taxes is through deferred annuities. Annuities accumulate income for distribution in the future. The primary advantage of annuities over IRAs is that there is generally no ceiling on the amount that may be deferred. Annuities are available from sources ranging insurance companies to stock brokers.

TAX-FREE INCOME

Municipal bonds offer the opportunity to accumulate tax-free income, but the 1986 Tax Act restricted tax-free status to those bonds which are supported by property taxes. These are general obligation bonds used by municipalities to fund various school and public works activities.

Should you buy the actual bonds or a bond fund? With many municipalities in financial trouble, the potential for bond default is real. You can reduce risk by purchasing bonds carrying ratings of A or better, or eliminate risk of default altogether by buying only insured bonds. Insured bonds, however, offer a half percentage point or so less interest than regular bonds.

Bond funds spread the risk of bond defaults by diversifying their holdings. A single bond fund will hold bonds from a wide assortment of communities. Generally, no more than 2% to 3% of their portfolios will consist of bonds from a single source, thus reducing risk should one or two issues default.

Does that mean that municipal bond funds are your best option? That depends on how actively you wish to manage your account. The net asset values of bond funds fluctuate with market conditions. If overall interest rates fall, net asset values rise and you enjoy an increase in capital. However, if interest rates rise, net asset values fall and your capital shrinks. Depending on the point to which interest rates rise and the mix of bonds in the fund's portfolio, you can experience an appreciable loss of capital. This goes double for high interest bond funds that invest primarily in lower grade bonds (bb or lower) or long term bonds (20- to 30-year maturity dates).

If you wish to invest in a fund, therefore, you'll need to keep an eye on the market. Still, a bond fund allows you to participate in tax-free investing for as little as $500. By contrast, bonds are sold in minimum lots of ten and will cost anywhere from $5,500 to more than $10,000, depending on the type, term, and interest rate of the bonds.

The primary advantage of bonds over funds is that if you buy high quality issues or insured bonds and hold them to maturity, your capital investment is guaranteed. Since the municipal bond market is thinly traded, it is wise to use a buy and hold strategy. The longer the term, the higher the interest rate. However, today when interest rates keep changing drastically, it is wise to invest in short to medium-term bonds (5- to 7-year maturity dates).

For safety, therefore purchase only bonds that are insured, rated A or better, or are issues of municipalities of which you have personal knowledge. Municipal bonds used to be regular recommendations for widow and orphan portfolios, but with many state and local governments on the brink of financial disaster extra caution is advised.

It's also wise to purchase only registered or zero-coupon bonds. Both avoid transaction charges involved in semi-annual redemptions of interest income from coupon-type bonds. These charges can amount to hundreds of dollars over the term of the bond.

A unit trust is another tax-free investment to consider. It combines the capital stability of individual bonds and the risk diversifying quality of bond funds. They are priced somewhere between bonds and bond funds starting at about $5,000.

Figure 9-2 gives you simple formulas you can use to determine the taxable equivalent of municipal bonds or bond funds. You'll need to use the formulas to see if the tax-free yield is really better than a taxable equivalent. All you need to know to use the formulas is your current tax rate.

MEDICAL AND MISCELLANEOUS DEDUCTIONS

The next group of deductions is subject to a floor percentage; in other words, only the amount beyond a percentage of your adjusted gross income is deductible. With medical expenses the floor is now 7.5%. The only news here is that elective surgery is no longer deductible. The most common elective surgery is cosmetic surgery.

For the following deductions, the floor is 2% of adjusted gross income:

Expenses of looking for a job are deductible if you stay in the same line of work, and it will not be your first job. You may

Figure 9-2: Tax-Free Equivalency Chart

Here's how to determine the taxable equivalent of a tax-free yield.

Find your tax bracket, divide the tax-free rate by the bracket divisor, and multiply your answer by 100.

Tax Bracket	Bracket Divisor
15%	85
28%	72
33%	67

Example: You need to know the taxable equivalent for a tax-free bond yielding 6.4%.

Taxable
Equivalent

6.4% ÷ 85 = .07529 x 100 = 7.53%
6.4% ÷ 72 = .08888 x 100 = 8.88%
6.4% ÷ 67 = .09552 x 100 = 9.55%

Note: To find the bracket divisor of any future bracket, subtract the bracket from 100.

deduct travel expenses and living costs plus any employment agency fees you have paid. Entertainment expenses to entertain former clients, customers, or colleagues are not deductible.

Moving expenses resulting from a job change are also deductible, if you move at least 35 miles from your former place of employment and remain in the new job for at least 39 weeks. For the self-employed or members of a partnership you must stay with your new position for at least 78 weeks. Moving expenses include:

1. 80% of your meals (travel and lodging are 100% deductible).
2. 80% of the cost of temporary lodging.
3. Car expenses at actual cost or 9¢ per mile.
4. The actual cost of moving personal possessions.
5. Expenses involved in selling, purchasing, or leasing a residence.

Uniforms and protective clothing are deductible, but the code is quite specific on what qualifies. Deductible uniforms are those which you must have to keep your job and which are not suitable for wear when you are not working. Protective clothing is anything designed to protect a worker from injury; clothes like coveralls used to protect regular clothing are non-deductible.

Union dues and professional subscriptions remain deductible. The code makes it very clear that while dues are deductible, special assessments for union benefits are not.

Non-reimbursed business expenses are deductible, but be careful. The IRS is very precise in its language on qualified deductions, and this is a deduction the IRS likes to challenge.

In years past, traveling professionals like salespeople could declare part of their homes to be a business office if they conducted business activities such as report-writing there. This deduction is now severely limited for employees. To deduct a home office you must be able to prove that *it is exclusively used as a principal place of business* or as a place to meet with patients, clients, or customers. Exclusive use means that the office space must not be used for personal purposes, as a den would be. Furthermore, you must be able to prove that the office is used for the convenience of your employer.

Employees rarely meet these conditions. An employee who may be excepted would be an outside salesman whose employer provides no office space or reimbursement for office space and who spends a substantial amount of time on paperwork at home.

Other business expenses such as entertaining and meals are deductible up to 80% of their cost. Travel and lodging are fully deductible. For 1991 the allowance for automobiles has been raised to 27.5¢ per mile. Note that, car phone expenses made for calls to clients or business associates while driving to the office are not deductible. They are considered commuting costs. Likewise, spouse expenses during business travel are not deductible.

Charitable contributions are another area the code defines precisely. In general, you can deduct charitable contributions equaling no more than 50% of your adjusted gross income. Excess donations, however, may be carried forward for the next five years. Keep in mind your projected income for the next five years if you plan to make large contributions you wish to deduct.

With all the fund-raising activities conducted by nonprofit organizations, the code also talks a lot about token gifts. Token gifts are small gifts and premiums given by charities for donations. They would include things like inexpensive pens, cameras, clocks, cassette players, and the like. Token gifts for public television, zoo, or museum donations must meet the test of being insubstantial in that:

1. they have a fair market value of the lower of $50 or 2% of the donation, *or*
2. the donation is at least $27.26, and the cost of the token items does not exceed $5.45.

Subscriptions to program guides and newsletters may qualify as a charitable contribution if the guides are not of commercial quality and are treated as having no fair market value or cost. Their primary purpose must be to inform members and they must not be available to nonmembers. Publications that incorporate paid articles and paid advertisements would be considered commercial quality and would be non-deductible.

Benefit tickets and tickets sold to theater events at a higher than regular price are deductible only in the amount of the difference. Donations to public or nonprofit college athletic scholarship programs to secure tickets to athletic events are deductible at 80% of the contribution. The cost of the tickets, however, is not deductible.

Capital Gains . . . no relief in sight! In 1987 the favorable treatment of capital gains was rescinded, and they have been since taxed at regular income rates to a maximum of 28%. However, the issue is constantly being debated by both Congress and the administration, and the rate could be raised or lowered from that point by the time you read this book. Capital losses, on the other hand, are subject to the "wash rule." What this means is if you sell securities to show a loss, you may not buy them back within 30 days.

THE EARNED INCOME CREDIT

You may have a check waiting for you from the Federal Government. If you have income of less than $20,264 and meet the household test qualifications, you may receive either a direct payment or a reduction in your taxes. To qualify you must be:

1. married and entitled to a dependency exemption for a child, *or*
2. be a qualifying widow, *or*
3. be a head of household (an unmarried child living with you need not be your dependent but a married child must be a dependent).

The credit schedule is 14% of your first $6,810. As your income rises, the credit is gradually reduced until it is phased out totally when you are earning $20,264.

HOW TO KEEP YOUR TAXES FROM GETTING BIGGER

Like it or not, politicians will always try to find new ways to raise taxes. However, you can take a few actions that will help you from paying any more taxes than necessary.

First, keep good records of deductible expenses. I find the easy way to keep track of them is to make a file at the beginning of the year for the current year's tax receipts. Include a couple of sheets of lined paper to record mileage and small miscellaneous expenses under $25. Then religiously write down expenses and deposit receipts for tax-deductible items into the file. When tax time arrives, all that'll be necessary to do will be some organizing and categorizing of your expenses.

Second, pay by check. Checks are the preferred documentation by the I.R.S. for charitable and other deductions. Charge card and cash receipts, however, are also acceptable.

Third, the reality of taxes is that you must pay them, but informed taxpayers are less likely to overpay. So make it a routine part of your wealth-building program to annually read or review tax booklets supplied by the I.R.S. and/or tax guides offered by commercial publishers. You can find both at your local public library. I realize that these booklets don't make exciting recreational reading, but they are your primary source of tax information and the place to find potential tax reductions. Also read newspaper and magazine tax columns, articles, and editorials. Both pending and proposed tax changes are regularly featured news items.

Be smart. The key to reducing your taxes is thorough knowledge and understanding of tax laws combined with the assistance of a qualified tax professional. Double your odds for success by using both sources.

Fourth, as citizens of this country we have direct control over how much tax we will pay by who we vote into office. Voting power gives us a choice. So if you don't like the current direction of our government, vote for those who better represent your viewpoint. Remember, in a typical national election, at best, only half of the eligible citizens vote. That means there are many who are not allowing their view to be expressed. Don't miss your opportunity—*Vote!*

CHAPTER **10**

Survival Solutions
for Credit Kamikazes

Earlier in the book I confessed to having been a credit card junkie. Well, I now confess that I was a credit kamikaze too! My careless use of credit nearly brought me, like those aviators of past Tora-Tora fame, into an explosive crash with reality. Fortunately, I was able to pull up and land. I lost the plane, but I managed to escape unhurt with a few possessions and a clean credit history.

In this country, there's so much to want and it's so easy to qualify to buy on credit. True, with the proper use of credit, you can lead a productive and complete life. The problem comes with wanting too much, too soon. Eventually the coveted item of our great desire is gone while its payments live on.

For others a credit problem may have been caused by a sudden loss of income or a personal tragedy. Whatever the cause, if you're in this situation you must find a solution.

Luckily for all of us our country's founding fathers prohibited imprisonment for debt, which was quite common in the Old World at that time. However, they made legal provisions for creditors to collect what is owed them. Although you can't be imprisoned for not paying your bills,[1] you can lose your wages through court-enforced garnishment and lose property

---

[1] *However, failure to pay federal income taxes and certain other Court ordered payments are punishable by imprisonment.*

and assets to court-mandated repossessions and liquidations. You can also suffer the aggravation, stress, and embarrassment of threatening letters, calls, and even visits. Always, the greatest loss of all is your loss of potential to become wealthy!

If you find yourself in this kind of situation don't feel alone. According to lawyer and author Janice Kosel, "Over the last three decades, the number of bankruptcies has risen over 2,000 percent. Now over a half a million bankruptcies are filed annually" (*Bankruptcy. Do It Yourself,* page 1).

But bankruptcy shouldn't be your first option. For me, it wasn't an acceptable solution at all. You may find it not to be an alternative for you either. There are many positive actions other than personal bankruptcy you can take to get yourself out of financial peril.

I feel that we have a moral obligation to pay our bills and that even when we're in trouble we should exhaust every possible alternative before seeking escape from our debts. However, I also know that there can be extenuating circumstances that make bankruptcy the only rational alternative. I present the following in this spirit and ask only you that you think deeply before taking any action.

FIRST STEPS

The first positive thing to do is to stop worrying and feeling guilty. That will get you nowhere. Resolve that, in time, you'll be out of debt. Also resolve that you'll never allow yourself to be in this situation again. Believe that there's a positive solution for your problems and with courage and clear thinking you can overcome your difficulties.

Now read on.

WHEN YOU CAN'T MAKE IT TO THE NEXT PAYCHECK

Start by cutting up your plastic. This may be very difficult for you because credit cards may have become cash substitutes. However, this is absolutely necessary, because continuing to use your cards is like throwing gasoline on a fire. To live without credit may mean you'll have to temporarily make do with the same clothes, shoes, and household goods. This is unfortunate but necessary.

Next look at your expenses. Find any pockets of unnecessary expense from the Friday night beer bash with the fellows to your Wednesday bowling league expenses and eliminate them. I realize that this is difficult and painful, but you're in a desperate situation and strong countermeasures are needed.

Call your creditors, tell them that you are trying to clear your debts, and ask for their help. Tell them that you have suspended further use of their cards until you have cleared your past debt. Also tell them that, in the future, you want to be more responsible in your use of credit. Try and get them to spread the payments over a longer time. Ask if there is some way they could arrange a lower rate of interest. If you're in a real bind, ask them if you can pay the interest only for a few months.

Most creditors will be helpful; it's in their best interest to be so. A few may be more difficult to deal with, especially if they have been burnt many times before. Don't sign any new agreement with a card company that uses your car, personal property, or real estate for collateral in exchange for a new payment schedule. Most credit card debt is unsecured, meaning that the creditor has no legal claim to your property in exchange for what is owed him. A new agreement could give him that right, so be careful.

If you own a home and home prices in your area have increased, you may have some equity you can borrow against. This would allow you to consolidate your credit card debt into one loan payable over a longer period and at a lower rate of interest (see Figure 10-1). Unlike your credit card debt, interest on this loan is fully deductible on your federal income tax.

A few caveats are in order. First, you'll most likely have to pay an application fee and closing costs to secure the home equity loan. You'll need to add these costs to the total interest charges over the life of the loan to compare which loan rate offers you the best deal. For example, a five-year 9.5% loan with a fee of $400 in closing costs and a $50 application fee is more expensive than a five-year 10% loan with no closing costs.

Second, once your credit card debt is removed and payments are lowered, you may be tempted to use your cards again for just a few things. *Don't!* The reason you had to take a home equity loan in the first place was that you got in trouble using credit cards. Operate on cash until the loan is paid off. By that time you'll have a much better understanding of the proper use of credit. If you find that you have cash left over, use it to build up your cash savings.

If you don't own a home or you do but not much equity has built up, you still can consolidate your credit card debt into a debt consolidation loan. This requires much judgment. There are many debt consolidation outfits looking for folks in financial trouble. These outfits end up soaking borrowers with sky-high interest and finance charges for secured property loans. If you default, they end up getting your car, boat, or any other collateral you used for the loan.

Look out: Some of these outfits come disguised as credit counselors. There is one financial credit counseling service that may help you, however. It is a non-profit organization sponsored by businesses, bankers, sales, and finance companies called The National Foundation for Consumer Credit. I have provided their

Figure 10-1: Debt Consolidation Chart

These tables compare credit debt to home equity loans of the same amount to demonstrate how payments, interest paid, or both may be lowered by consolidating debt into one home equity loan. In this example, 5- and 7-year home equity loans offer both lower payments and interest than either credit card payment schedule. A 10-year term, however, offers significantly lower payments than either credit card schedule, but only lower total interest paid than the credit card minimum payment schedule.

Table A
Credit Card Payments and Interest: Minimum Payment Schedule

Amount Charged	Annual % Card Int.	Monthly Payment Range	Interest Paid Over 5 Years	Bal. Rem. After 5 Yrs.
$3,500	15.5%	$122.50-45.72	$2,403.55	$1,306.13
1,850	18.5	64.75-40.89	1,279.80	681.02
2,235	21.8	78.23-49.57	1,558.56	839.61
1,645	21.8	57.58-36.58	1,147.13	617.97
$9,230	N.A.	$204.16/mo. avg	$6,389.04	$3,444.73

Table B
Credit Card Payments and Interest: Uniform Payment Schedule

Amount Charged	Annual % Card Int.	Monthly Payment	Interest Paid Over 5 Years	Bal. Rem. After 5 Yrs.[1]
$3,500	15.5%	$122.50	$1,426.25	$ .00
1,850	18.5	64.75	751.82	.00
2,235	21.8	78.23	916.56	.00
1,645	21.8	57.58	674.16	.00
$9,230	N.A.	$323.06/mo. avg	$3,768.79	$ .00

Table C
Consolidation of Debt: Using a Home Equity Loan

Loan Term	Amount Borrowed	Interest Rate	Monthly Payment	Total Interest Paid[2]
5 years	$9,230	10.5%	$200.32	$2,285.34
7 years	9,230	10.5	157.14	3,555.09
10 years[3]	9,320	10.5	125.76	5,771.13

Notes:
1. All debt would be paid off in 42 months at this payment level.
2. Excludes application fees which average, in the Chicago metropolitan area, around $250 and closing costs that range from $50 to $150.
3. Fifteen-year term home equity loans are also available.

address and telephone number in the "Sources" section in the back of this book. This organization wants to help you figure out if and how you can repay your debts.

EARNINGS ALTERNATIVES

Another way of getting out of debt is simply by earning more. The most obvious way is to take a second or part-time job. Older children can help. I can hear the screaming already. Folks, the ME generation bit is over. The time for the WE generation is long overdue! In the old days (40 or so years ago) everyone helped out. In dire times everyone should pitch in. Baby-sitting money and paper routes can all contribute. Please, though, use a little common sense. It's far more important for your kids to spend time studying than flipping burgers to get Mom and Dad out of hock. However, if they already have a job, then they should help their family. They can make a direct cash contribution or they can take over their own personal expenses like buying their own clothes or lunches or paying school and athletic fees.

Have an extra room? Take in a border. A rather well-off friend of mine has shared his three-bedroom condo with a college student for years. He enjoys the company and has been able to put a considerable amount of the income away for his retirement. For even greater income, check with your municipality or zoning authority to see if you can turn that unused basement into a garden flat.

Start a part-time maintenance business doing minor repairs, painting, washing windows, cleaning gutters, mowing lawns, or delivering groceries. In my area these jobs can't be filled because no one's available. You can make $25 to $35 an hour for tasks like this. Run a small classified ad in the neighborhood paper of a wealthier suburb and watch what happens.

DO A DONALD TRUMP . . . SELL YOUR ASSETS

Got a boat or sports car you can barely afford? Expensive golf clubs, fishing tackle, collector guns, stamps, coins, or antiques? They're doing you no good if you're so financially strapped you can't enjoy them. Sell them now before you're forced to. When you're not under pressure, you're in a better frame of mind to negotiate price than if you're desperate. Whatever you do don't run despondent-sounding ads: "Must sell immediately." "Need cash—must sell 1965 Corvette." This tells any potential buyer you're in trouble and will take the lowest price. Likewise, when folks come to buy your treasure, don't look like you've just lost your mother. Your depression will cost you in the price they offer. Act as if you're tired of your things . . . you need more room, you have a new hobby, whatever works.

You can always buy these kind of things again. In fact, when you really get going, you'll be able to buy much better things. I know how hard it is to sell things you really enjoy. During my last financial crisis, I found it very hard to part with my red roadster. During hard times it had provided an escape for me. I'd roll down the top and ride through the countryside. The purr of its mellow exhaust pipes seemed to melt my troubles. I was so attached to it, before I sold it, I photographed it from every imaginable angle. It was a waste of good film.

If you're close to losing some property to creditors, it would be wise to convert it to exempt property, property that cannot be taken by creditors even if they take legal action against you. This will be dealt with in detail in the next section on bankruptcy.

WHEN HIDING YOUR CAR WON'T HELP

A famous millionaire tells the story of how he used to sit in a dark office during the 1930s Depression so that the repossessors would think he had already gone home and would not follow him to where he had hidden his car.

The point of the story is to illustrate when it's time to think about bankruptcy. As I said before, I feel personal bankruptcy is a last resort. Some of the books and articles I read disagree with me. Instead, they portray bankruptcy as a financial tool you can use to get out of burdensome debt. One book went so far as to quote the Bible.

In my mind, the time to think about personal bankruptcy is when, despite your best efforts, nothing else has helped. Your wages have been or will be garnished, creditor lawsuits have been or are about to be filed, your property is about to be repossessed or sold for debt or back taxes. In short, you are in serious trouble and have nowhere else to turn.

Personal bankruptcy will eliminate all debt except that which is considered *non-dischargeable*. Non-dischargeable debt includes:

1. Alimony or child support.
2. Student loans.[1]
3. State or federal income taxes that were not due within the past three years.
4. Auto accident claims where the driver was drunk or reckless. In contrast, claims from accidents entailing ordinary negligence are dischargeable.
5. Fines.
6. Debts obtained using fraudulent statements. This includes loan applications with misstatements about income, amount of debt, or listed assets.
7. Property obtained by fraud. This includes items obtained with checks that were returned for insuffi-

---

[1] *There are some exceptions. Like if the loans first became due over five years ago or if the loans "impose an undue hardship." However, to be certain check on current rulings with an attorney.*

cient funds and credit purchases within 40 days of filing for bankruptcy.

Contrary to what you may think, you'll be allowed to keep a portion of your assets including equity in your home, car, savings, and investments. This is called exempt property. The purpose of exempting certain items from liquidation for debt is to help the bankrupt person get a fresh start. A bankrupt person has a choice of using the federal exemption system or the one used by the state in which he resides. The following is a sample of what is exempted under the federal system:

1. Equity in a residence of any kind up to $7,500.
2. A motor vehicle with an equity up to $1,200.
3. Unemployment compensation, disability income, health insurance benefits, Social Security benefits, Veterans benefits.
4. $500 equity in jewelry.
5. $4,000 cash value of life insurance.
6. 75% of wages earned but not paid during the last 30 days.

Assets that exceed the exempted limits will be used to pay debts owed. Non-exempt property and assets will be liquidated and the proceeds allocated among the creditors. It is therefore in your best interest to transfer any assets you can to exempted categories before you file.

In a straight bankruptcy, any debt remaining after property and asset assignment will be discharged (forgiven) except those which are non-dischargeable. However, when loans are secured by property, the property must be returned to the creditor in exchange for debt forgiveness. You may be allowed to keep the item if you agree to pay an amount acceptable to the creditor. Unsecured debt (like credit card debt) will be completely discharged or erased.

When you file, all creditor collection or repossession efforts, even IRS actions, will be suspended. Be careful when you file, however, because income received on or about the filing date may be taken for your creditor settlement. Examples include tax refunds, 75% of any unpaid wages, insurance settlements, and inheritances received up to six months after filing.

Chapter 11 of the Bankruptcy Code is the one we hear the most about. It's in the news daily. "Yesterday Big Tell, Inc. filed Chapter 11. . . ." Chapter 11 offers individuals who own small businesses advantages too. Like other portions of the code it pays off a portion of one's debts via liquidation of assets. The size of the pay off is worked out through meetings with creditors and is approved by majority vote of each category of creditors. However, it also allows the individual to continue running the business.

Chapter 13 differs in that a debtor is allowed to keep all property while paying off debts in whole or part over a three-year period. Like other bankruptcy procedures, after filing creditors are prohibited from harassing debtors.

THE DOWNSIDE OF BANKRUPTCY

The good side of bankruptcy is that a portion or all of your debts will be forgiven. You'll retain some of your assets and you get a fresh start free from debt.

There is a bad side, however. For one thing you will lose some of your assets. How much depends how much you have. Also you'll most likely have to live a credit-less life for ten years, because credit-reporting services are allowed to keep a record of bankruptcies for that length of time. Once your debts are erased, even if you want to clear things up with your former creditors, you cannot do so unless your offer is court-approved.

Bankruptcy can give you a fresh start when all your other options have been expended, but you may file only once every six years. So use it prudently.

CHAPTER **11**

Attitudes
for Success

For many years I attributed my financial problems to the inability to make enough money. No part-time or second job ever brought in enough additional money to help. I blamed difficulties on my former profession, but a change in careers didn't help—even though my income more than doubled as a result of the change. I just couldn't earn enough money to keep me from going further in debt. Like a donkey chasing a carrot on a stick, the harder I worked the less I had to show for my efforts. I was unaware that, all the while, my lifestyle was increasing along with my income. This continued until the whole thing came apart about three years later.

DO YOU HAVE AN EARNING OR SPENDING PROBLEM?

Up to that time, I hadn't realized that earnings were never the source of my problems. Mine was a spending problem. I didn't use my money wisely. I bought too much too soon and bought exclusively on credit. I rarely bought on sale, never saved for savings sake, and in general had a consuming lifestyle. Eventually I reached the point that half or more my gross income went to installment payments of one kind or another. Needless to say, the amount of interest I paid was disgraceful.

I justified my extravagance because all the interest charges, at that time, were tax-deductible. Fantastic thinking, huh? Waste thousands of dollars on interest to get a couple of hundred back in tax refunds.

Getting wealthy and staying wealthy begin and end with your attitude. Attitude determines your direction. Attitude defines how long it will take you to fulfill your dreams. Attitude opens your eyes to the unseen opportunities that are in your own backyard.

You may find it a little difficult to accept that just by changing your mind, you can change your life, but it's true! Books are filled with examples, but it's been the living examples that I've met that have proven this reality to me.

THE THIRD TIME'S A CHARM

Years ago I met an interesting fellow who taught me just how important attitude and determination are to success. His story significantly altered my viewpoint and that's why I want to share it with you.

I met him shortly after I graduated from college. I had just started a new job as a teaching principal in a small-town elementary school. This was quite an achievement for me at that time and I was feeling proud.

It was a few days before the school was to open and I was setting up my classroom and office. The District Superintendent stopped by to tell me that an exterminator would be around to spray the building and that I should let him in.

Around ten o'clock the next day a van bearing the name of the extermination company pulled up and a man a couple of years older than me jumped out. I let him in the building. Since I had little left to do, I followed him around and talked with him as he worked. He was clad in brown work clothes and carried a large canister of bug spray; I felt both sorry for him and a little superior at the same time.

"How much can a guy like this make?" I thought. "Two or three bucks an hour at best," I concluded. My thoughts were interrupted with his words. He told me he had a wife and kids and that at one time he had a job like mine. Upon hearing this I was overwhelmed with pity. My thoughts rambled on, "This poor schmoe lost his teaching job and couldn't find another. Look at what kind of job he had to take just to survive."

These egotistical thoughts came crashing in on me when he told me he owned his exterminating company. I sought some salvation for my pride by asking him how big his operation was. He told me that he had three fully-equipped vans, four full-time workers, a secretary, an office, in short the works. I was embarrassed for thinking such stupid thoughts, but now my curiosity was screaming for satisfaction. I asked him if he had taught chemistry, thinking that there was a natural link between his past career and his present business. He told he had taught accounting.

I could no longer hold back so I asked him outright how he decided on this business. He said he found the opportunity by accident. He was looking for an exterminator for his own home and had discovered that the nearest one was some 40 miles away in another county. He reasoned that a county the size of ours could easily support one, possibly even two, extermination businesses.

Since he didn't know anything about the business, he decided that the best way to learn would be from the suppliers of extermination chemicals and equipment. He got the name and address of a supplier from the back of a chemical spray left behind by the exterminator who visited his home. He called the company and made them an unusual offer: He explained that he was a teacher; since he had the summer off, he offered to work free if they would teach him the business. The company agreed.

He left his family and spent the next summer at the chemical supplier's headquarters in a city 1,000 miles from his home. The chemical supplier was so impressed with his plan, proposed market, and spirit that at the end of the summer the supplier extended him a $75,000 line of credit for chemicals and equipment. The rest was history.

I asked him if he ever feared not making it, going bankrupt, and not being able to secure a teaching job again. His answer shocked me. He told me he wasn't afraid because he already had had two other businesses fail. He said that he didn't consider them total flops, though, because he had learned from his experience. Based on that experience, he was sure this business would work. He concluded by saying that, even if it failed, he could always try something else.

His story inspired me to think about my own future. Here was a guy who had failed twice before and wasn't crushed by the experience. More important, he wasn't afraid of failing again. He was a guy like me, a former teacher with little capital. Until that time I thought that you needed gobs of money to start a business. It astounded me to discover that just a good idea, a plan, and the right kind of attitude could make a dream come true. Even more startling to me was that you could fail many times and still enjoy success, as long as you didn't allow failure to defeat you!

THE ATTITUDES FOR FINANCIAL SUCCESS

Like the man in the story, you must have the right attitude to become wealthy on a paycheck. You must become financially mature and learn life's number one financial rule: No one can have it all. To violate this rule is to invite financial ruin. The rule does not discriminate. You are affected by it no matter how much you earn or how much money you have. The rule underlines the importance of learning to be satisfied and thankful with what you do have. There's always more to want.

You must also develop an attitude of fiscal responsibility, become accountable for your spending, learn how to discipline yourself, be able to say NO to yourself. You must learn how to approach all financial matters, from buying your morning cup of coffee to the purchase of a new car, in a logical, calculated way. Never, ever buy anything on impulse again, no matter how tempting it may be.

Financial maturity means never again being intimidated by financial concepts, products, or language. It means not trying to bluff your way through life, but rather making conscious efforts to learn about the things of which you have little knowledge. It means making the pursuit of wealth and self-improvement a way of life, making it as regular a part of your daily life as brushing your teeth.

It also means keeping things in perspective. All good things take time and energy and will undoubtedly require a greater struggle than you'd like. You will have some disappointments and failures. The right attitude will allow you to pick yourself up and start again, keeping your eyes open for opportunity even disguised as failure, as it was for me.

The right attitude also means, being realistic in our financial expectations for our children. They mirror our actions. If we spend our money foolishly, we can't expect our kids to be great savers. We must teach them by our example.

THE SUCCESSES OF OTHERS

I know it is particularly difficult to see the successes of others while you're struggling. It's very human to become jealous and angry. "Why them and not me?" is a natural response. Natural, yes, but self-destructive, because it focuses on what you *don't* have. It keeps you focused on failure.

A more positive and realistic attitude is "If they can do it, So Can I!" Instead of being jealous, be inspired. Their success proves that it's still possible to succeed in this great country of ours. Understand that successful folks are just like you; they don't have any greater powers or innate abilities than you have.

To help you keep the right attitude, read positive thinking books and the biographies of successful people like Lee Iaccoca, the President of Chrysler Motors, or Ray Kroc, founder of McDonald's. Great success stories and positive thoughts are integral to keeping you in an achieving frame of mind.

It's vitally important to believe in yourself and your ability to change your life. Decide today, that your life as a member of the working poor is over. Vow that you will use the *guerilla savings* techniques, will diary your expenses, get out of debt, make better purchases, develop an annual budget, create a five-year plan, begin research on investing, and start a savings program. Take action! Get rich!

THE LAW OF RETURNING COMPENSATION

There's a philosophical and metaphysical truth: You'll receive that which you believe in most. The Eastern religions call this *The Law of Returning Compensation.* What it means is that you'll be rewarded according to your strongest beliefs and actions. You may be rewarded, however, negatively as well as positively, depending upon which thoughts and actions dominate. So take care of your thoughts!

It is also part of the Christian religion: "For whatever a man sows, this he will also reap" (Galatians 6:7) or "Therefore I say to you, all things for which you pray and ask, believe that you have received them and they shall be granted you" (Mark 11:24).

If you don't wish to accept the spiritual side of this concept, at least see the logic of it. When you're mentally attuned to money-making opportunities, you're more likely to see them. How many thousands of other people in that same county also had to call for exterminators outside the county but never saw the opportunity the former teacher realized. If they did see it, it's apparent that they didn't either appreciate its value or know how to take advantage of their discovery. This man saw it because his mind was fixed on business opportunities. He believed strongly in his ability to eventually succeed.

The same holds true for the pursuit of wealth. Believe with all your heart that you can succeed and take appropriate action.

GO FOR IT!

This may be the end of this book, but it is the beginning of a new life for you. What I have given you in these pages is a program that has worked for me and my family. My enthusiasm is that of one who has learned these things the hard way: An ordinary guy like you who frets and sweats. A working person from an ordinary middle-class family. A guy who has worked for everything he owns. A person who truly knows that it is possible for anyone to be better off than they are today.

Because I'm just an ordinary person I feel qualified to say, "If we can do it, anyone can!" I wish you great financial success, health, and the hope for a better, richer life.

It's up to you now. *Go For It!*

Suggested Reading

FINANCIAL / INVESTING

General / Basic Information on Investing

Daniels, Lorna M., *Business Information Sources*. Berkley, CA: University of California Press, 1985. A unique reference to business statistical sources and investment references. Provides a synopsis of the types of information that can be found in the source that is listed.

Graham, Benjamin, *The Intelligent Investor: A Book of Practical Counsel*, 4th rev. ed., New York: Harper & Row, 1986.

_____ , *Graham and Dodds's Security Analysis*, New York: McGraw Hill, 1988.

Selected Topics

American Association of Individual Investors, *The Individual Investor's Guide to No-Load Mutual Funds*, 10th ed., Chicago: International Publishing Corporation, 1991.

Burgauer, James, *Do-It-Yourself Investment Analysis*, Chicago: International Publishing Corporation, 1990.

Daily, Glenn S., *The Individual Investor's Guide to Low-Load Insurance Products*, Chicago: International Publishing Corporation, 1990.

Lamb, Robert and Stephen P. Rappaport, *Municipal Bonds,* 2nd ed., New York: McGraw Hill, 1987.

Nichols, Donald R., *The Personal Investor's Complete Book of Bonds,* Chicago: Longman Financial Services Publishing, 1989.

Investment References You Should Know About

Federal government publications are available from the U.S. General Services Administration, Consumer Information Center, Department RW, Pueblo, Colorado, 81009. Write for a free catalog of about 200 titles, many of them also free.

Standard and Poors Corporation, Stock Reports. Provides financial data on hundreds of U.S. corporations on the New York Stock Exchange and Over the Counter markets. Reports provide detailed information offering a business summary, recent developments, balance sheet, and per share data, capitalization, dividends, etc. Data is analyzed for the past five years. Unique to S&P Reports are assets to liabilities ratios and data on net income before taxes, effective tax rate, net income, and cash flow.

Value Line Investment Survey. An investment service that regularly analyzes and reports on 1,700 companies in 95 industries. Statistics, charts, and brief explanations are updated on an alternating basis so that information on each company in each industry is revised quarterly. The easy-to-read one page per company analyses are packed with data including an ll year statistical history on 22 key investment factors. Unique to *Value Line* are 3-year to 5-year stock price projections, ratings on timeliness, safety, company financial strength, stock price stability, price growth persistence, beta, and earnings predictability. Also included is a weekly "Summary & Index" and "Selection & Opinion"offering commentary on financial outlook and investment advice. I find *Value Line* to be a reliable source of conservative investment information.

Inspirational Books

Dyer, Wayne W., *Your Erroneous Zones,* New York: Avon Books, 1977.

_____ , *Pulling Your Own Strings,* New York: Avon Books, 1977.

Hill, Napoleon, *Think and Grow Rich,* New York: Hawthorn Books, E.P. Dutton, Inc, 1972.

Hull, Raymond, *How To Get What You Want,* New York: Funk & Wagnalls, a Division of Reader's Digest Books, 1969.

Maltz, Maxwell, *Psychocybernetics,* North Hollywood, CA: Wilshire Book Company, 1960.

Mandino, Og, *The Greatest Salesman in the World,* New York: Bantam Books, 1968.

Peale, Norman Vincent, *The Power of Positive Thinking,* New York: Fawcett Crest Books, 1952.

Sher, Barbara, *Wishcraft—How to Get What You Really Want,* New York: Ballantine Books, 1983.

Selected Biographies

Ash, Mary Kay, *The Success Story of America's Most Dynamic Businesswoman,* New York: Harper & Row, 1987.

Hilton, Conrad, *Be My Guest,* New York: Prentice Hall, a Division of Simon & Schuster, Inc., 1957.

Iococca, Lee, *Iococca, an autobiography,* New York: Bantam, 1984.

Kroc, Ray, *Grinding It Out,* New York: Regnery, 1977.

Obrien, Robert, *Marriot: The J. Willard Marriott Story,* Salt Lake City, UT: Deseret Book Co., 1977.

Sources

BOOKS

American Association of Individual Investors, *1990 Personal Tax & Financial Planners Guide,* Newark, NJ: Prentice-Hall Publishing, 1990.

The Big Black Book, New York: Boardroom Reports, Inc., 1987, pages 317, 318, 377, 477.

The Book of Inside Information, New York: Boardroom Reports, Inc., 1987, page 5.

Kosel, Janice, *Bankruptcy. Do It Yourself,* 4th ed., Berkley, CA: Nolo Press, 1985.

Lasser, J.K., *J.K. Lasser's 1991 Complete Tax Savers Guide for 1990 Returns,* New York: 1990.

Statistical Abstracts of the United States, Washington: 1989, "Top Wealth Holders with Gross Assets of $325,000 or more by size of net worth and sex," page 463.

MAGAZINES

Egan, Jack and Anne Kates Smith, "It'll Just Hurt a Little," *U.S. News and World Report,* November 12, 1990, page 30.

Fisher, Kenneth L., "Don't Sell America Short," *Forbes,* June 11, 1990, page 232.

Forbes, Malcolm S., "How to Help the Sluggish Economy," *Forbes,* July 23, 1990, page 19.

"Key to Growth: No New Taxes," *Nation's Business,* Vol. 78, No. 9, September, 1990, pages 21-22.

Khalat, Roula, "America Bashing," *Forbes,* November 26, 1990, page 171.

Lee, Susan, "Too Early for a Party," *Forbes,* July 23, 1990, page 171.

"Preserving Jobs & Productivity," *Nation's Business,* Vol. 78, No. 9, September 1990, page 42.

"Read the Lobbyist's Lips: Tax the Other Guy," *Newsweek,* Vol. 116, No. 3, July 16, 1990, page 42.

Sherrid, Pamela, "Money Matters of the Mind," *U.S. News & World Report,* Vol. 109, No. 5, July 30, 1990, page 53.

_____ , "The New Old Case for Munis," *U.S. News & World Report,* December 17, 1990, page 116.

Slovic, Paul, "Informing and Educating the Public about Risk," *Risk Analysis,* Vol. 6, No. 4, 1986, page 407.

Smith, Anne Kates, "How to Think About Your Home," *U.S. New & World Report,* November 12, 1990, pages 70-72.

"Social Security: The Bottom Line," *Forbes,* January 23, 1989, page 96.

Wiener, Leonard, "Juggle Now, Save Later," *U.S. News & World Report,* November 12, 1990, pages 86-88.

OTHER: CREDIT COUNSELING

National Foundation for Consumer Credit, 8701 Georgia Avenue, #507, Silver Springs, MD 20910. (301) 589-5600.

Books for Guerilla Savers

VALUE AVERAGING: The Safe and Easy Strategy for Higher Investment Returns
by Michael E. Edleson

This innovative investment strategy addresses the age-old problem all investors face: how to "buy low" and then "sell high" to build real wealth safely and consistently over time. Explains easy and effective "mechanical" ways to build wealth at lower costs and with higher returns. Shows you how to make the buying and selling of stock nearly automatic, relieving you of emotional anxiety and the need for market-timing skills; recommends investments suited for value averaging; tells how to avoid taxes, transaction costs, and other hassles; and demonstrates how to use value averaging for specific goals such as your retirement or kids' college tuition. Full of useful tables, graphs, examples, and simulations, Edleson even walks you through value averaging on your hand calculator (and shows how to set up a spreadsheet program) so you can easily put the safe and easy strategy—value averaging—to work today for higher investment returns.

216 pages   ISBN: 0-942641-27-2   **$22.95**

Retirement Planning: THE REAL MID-LIFE CRISIS
by Duane D. Freese

This down-to-earth guide takes you step by step from where you are now to where you want to be 10, 15, 25 years from now. Written for all who have been too busy living to plan for retirement, it helps you see what you have now and decide what you want in retirement. Tells how to build and invest your nest egg, to sort out and maximize your sources of retirement income, to figure how much money you really need in retirement, to analyze your saving, spending, budgeting skills. Plus it gives you the lowdown on Social Security and pensions, ways to get started in "safe" and "growth" investing, tips on choosing a lawyer, executor, stock broker, and easy-to-use forms to track your budgeting, savings, investments, and taxes to secure your financial future.

168 Pages   ISBN: 0-942641-25-6   **$17.50**

Order IPC books at your bookstore, or use the coupon below, or call 312/943-7354

Ship to: _____

Address: _____

State, Zip: _____

Make checks payable to International Publishing, Corp., Inc., or

Charge Visa/Mastercard Number_____ Expire date_____

Signature: _____

Send me your brochure describing all IPC titles for guerilla savers _____

Quantity	Title	Price
_____	VALUE AVERAGING: The Safe/Easy Investment Strategy	_____
_____	Retirement Planning: THE REAL MID-LIFE CRISIS	_____

Send to	**International Publishing Corp., Inc.**	Shipping/Handling	$1.50 _____
	625 N. Michigan Ave., Suite 1920	Add IL Tax (7%)	_____
	Chicago, IL 60606	Total	_____

Full Payment must accompany coupon orders.